AF651215

Concept Publishing Co. (P) Ltd.
₹ 250/-
SINCE - 1974

TECHNOLOGY AND SOCIAL TRANSFORMATION

TECHNOLOGY AND SOCIAL TRANSFORMATION

The Case of the Hirakud Multi-Purpose Dam Project in Orissa

BALGOVIND BABOO
Associate Professor/Deputy Director
Academic Staff College
Jawaharlal Nehru University, New Delhi

CONCEPT PUBLISHING COMPANY, NEW DELHI 110059

All right reserved. No part of this work may be reproduced, stored in a retrieval system or transmitted, in any form or by any means, electronic, mechanical, photocopying, recording or otherwise, without the prior permission of the copyright owner.

The Indian Council of Social Science Research gave the financial support towards the publication of this work. However, the responsibility for the contents of the book — facts, opinions, conclusions, etc. — is entirely that of the author and not of the ICSSR.

ICSSR Consultant: S.C. Dube

ISBN 81-7022-427-6

First Published 1992

© Balgovind **Baboo** (*b.* 1955)

Published and Printed by
Ashok Kumar Mittal
Concept Publishing Company
A/15-16, Commercial Block Mohan Garden
NEW DELHI 110059 (India)

Lasertypeset by
Microtech Advance Printing System (Pvt.) Ltd.
H-13, Bali Nagar
NEW DELHI 110015

Dedicated this work to

My father who marvelled at the positive aspects of the Hirakud dam without knowing its long-term nuances and social costs.

PREFACE

During 1980-81, when I was doing fieldwork relating to economic exchanges in different types of villages in Orissa, I observed that in four out of the six villages that I studied, there were a few households who were identified as *budi anchalar loka* (reservoir oustees) and who themselves told that they were not properly integrated in the village and that their economic status had been completely shattered as a result of displacement. Given the limitation of a Ph.D thesis, which I was pursuing then, I could not explore in detail the rehabilitational aspects of these oustees. A post-Doctoral Fellowship from the ICSSR during Aug. 1986 - July 1988 and an extra-ordinary leave for two years from the M.D.University, Rohtak, enabled me to pursue this problem further. I am thankful to both the organisations.

The sections that follow this brief preface discuss the problems and prospects of the reservoir oustees in the context of development and displacement in general, and that of the Hirakud dam oustees in particular. It is about historical conditioning of the Hirakud dam, about peoples' resistance to such an event, the several processes in the construction of the dam, about displacement, rehabilitation and reconstruction of life of the oustees and the 'hosts' in a somewhat culturally incongruous situation. Keeping in mind that construction of dam would be an on-going phenomenon in India, the study emphasises certain issues pertaining to policy measures and alternative forms of development.

I am grateful to Prof. T.K. Oommen, who encouraged me to work on the present theme and later critically commented on the first draft of the project report. This book is a revised version of that report. I am thankful to the staff members at Centre for Science and Environment, and Participatory Research in Asia, Delhi; to Dr. Kashyap Mankodi at Centre for Social Studies, Surat, to Dr. Michael Cernia at World Bank, to Prof. Satish Saberwal at JNU, to Prof. Andre Beteille at Delhi School of Economics, and to Prof. Nilakantha Rath at GIPE, Pune, who provided valuable material or commented and suggested improvements to my project proposal. I must place on records my thanks to Prof. Kuldeep Mathur at JNU who has been a continuous source of encouragement. I am also thankful to the editors of Economic and Political Weekly, Indian Journal of Social Sciences, Social Action, Man in India, and Sociologus, who have published portions of this work in their Journals.

My wife Sabita and son Sabyasachi had to bear with my long absence during fieldwork in different parts of Orissa. I am thankful to them to have excused me for my negligence to them. Finally, my gratitude knows no bounds for the respondents — both oustees and natives — and my hosts in the field, who provided me with valuable information and timely hospitalities hoping that my study would ease up their difficulties and would be helpful guide for future dam oustees in India.

November 1991 BALGOVIND BABOO

CONTENTS

LIST OF TABLES, CHART AND APPENDICES

Tables

Chart

Appendices

1

PEOPLE VERSUS DAM IN THE OVERALL CONTEXT OF TECHNOLOGY VERSUS SOCIAL TRANSFORMATION

For a long time in history man marvelled at the natural catastrophies and calamities — flood, drought, thunder, cyclone, volcanic eruption, glacial movement, wild fires, pestilences, etc. — with awe. He dazed at scorching heat, pelting rains and biting cold. On top of it he was completely dependent on nature for food, drink, clothing, shelter, implements, light and shower. Man had little control over physical environment. His dependence on nature, for his survival and sustenance, made him worship various elements of nature and it also shaped his material and non-material culture. During ravages of nature man simply succumbed to it or had to flee hundreds of miles away. Over thousands of years man gradually improved his technology. However, the dependence on nature was still so pervasive that right until the Second World War, the "deterministic" school of Human Geography prevailed in man's thinking.[1] It would not, however, be an exaggeration to say that technology has revolutionised our life during the last three hundred years or so. Technological innovation is probably the most important factor of modernisation in agriculture, industry, and cultural refinement — in all parts of the world, irrespective of religio-political credo.[2] Unlike earlier times when people moved en mass considerable distance to get rid of the wrath of nature, in today's world people move intranationally or internationally due to voluntary economic pursuits, compulsive political/religious/economic factors or man-made planned 'adventures' like large scale industry, mining, urbanisation, irrigation projects, power plants and military bases, etc. The mass movement of population has been engineered by man's increasing thirst for comfort, conquest over nature, population pressure, and made feasible by advances in transportation. Such compulsive and planned movement of population has led to an ecological crisis in most parts of the world, reshaping as it does the hills and forests, settlements and agricultural land, rivers and lakes, and in sum the flora, fauna and the landscape. Such "possibilistic" outlook has endangered the intrinsic unity of man and environment. The basic idea behind such a move is 'development' 'progress', or 'modernisation', which has become a fad and which is essentially a value loaded concept.[3]

Displacement, consequent upon development, may be sponsored or self-financed, voluntary or involuntary, immediate or gradual, small scale or large scale, to nearby or distant place, and to similar or dissimilar locales, etc. A typology of displacement, as presented in Chart-I, can be built taking some such factors into account.[4] Return to normalcy or rehabilitation will also be different depending on the interplay of such factors as well as on the nature of population. Evacuation and rehabilitation of industrial-urban population will necessarily be different from agricultural population.

Agriculture is dependent as much on soil, sunshine, and air as on rainfall or irrigation. In ancient times, man used rain water for agriculture — directly or in stored form — and used the stored water of tanks, ponds, lakes, rivers and sea for domestic, urban-industrial and agricultural use. Several types of lifting, pumping and direct flow methods were used. When population and later industrial-urbanisation increased and man's need for water increased manifold for various uses, surface water had to be stored in large quantities and for a longer period. The unpredictable, irregular and diffuse nature of rainfall leading to drought and flood, and thereby causing loss of life and property, led people to think of ways to store water in a big way. Similarly, after the industrial revolution, generation of power for industrialisation and domestic consumption prompted people to think in terms of cheaper hydro-electric power. All these factors alongwith the improvement in machine and building technology led to the construction of sizeable earthen and concrete dams.

Man has been constructing dams since the beginning of historical era. In India, there are hundreds of large, medium and small dams, and hundreds are under construction and in planning stage. The total lake area covered by these projects has been increasing over years and partly shown in Table 1.1. The amount spent in dam construction in India during different plans is provided in Table 1.2. These figures give us the impression that over years the expenditure on dams and

CHART - I

A TYPOLOGY OF DISPLACEMENT AND REHABILITATION

Agencies of Rehabilitation

Nature of Displacement	SELF/GROUP	GOVERNMENT	OTHER AGENCIES
VOLUNTARY	1. Intra-national or international migration for achieving higher objectives. It is expected to end up in proper rehabilitation since the migrant population ascertains the congeniality of the new situation and is in a position to calculate the costs and the benefits before displacement.	2. Long-term migration, sometimes resulting in habitation in the new place because of government services. It is expected to result in proper rehabilitation because of reasons provided in the first category.	3. Long-term migration due to the offer of private and voluntary agencies sometimes resulting in the settlement of the migrants. It might end up in proper rehabilitation because of reasons provided in the first category.
PARTLY COMPULSORY	4. Displacement of population to nearby similar localities due to deforestation, pollution of river and atmosphere, and developmental projects. Nobody compels peoples to move but they do so because their source of livelihood is cut off or curtailed or because the area does not become habitable for human beings. Rehabilitation may be painful unless sources of livelihood are restored, and unless the host community cooperates.	5. Displacement due to mineral extraction & industrialisation by government. People are rehabilitated in the vicinity of the 'field' for meeting labour demands. Rehabilitation is usually in the form of employment to at least one member in the family primarily in the unskilled/semi-skilled jobs. Sometimes developmental project requiring acquisition of agricultural land only (as in the case of sub-mergence) also results in partial displacement but most of the people can stay back or shift to a new locality because of new opportunities, and provided by the government.	6. Displacement due to mineral extraction & industrialisation by private agencies. Rehabilitation in the vicinity of the 'field' for meeting labour demands, which might not be very satisfactory.
COMPULSORY	7. Sometimes individual households or social groups arrange for self-rehabilitation in different pre-settled similar localities because no outside help is extended or that they are not satisfied with the help available from the government or other agencies. This may happen due to developmental or defence projects and even due to condition of political and religious oppression, as in the case of the refugees.	8. Sometimes government provide for the rehabilitation of people displaced due to developmental projects or persecution from a foreign country. The rehabilitation in planned laid out colonies, sometimes in dis-similar locals with heterogeneous population, destroys the community structure. Rehabilitation by enblock transplantation does not destroy community structure, but non-availability of matching facilities sometimes obstructs this plan.	9. Dissatisfied with the governmental scheme of rehabilitation sometimes, voluntary organisations may take to this measure in cooperation with the people and the government. In the absence of 'legitimacy' of these agencies, there may be problems of coordinating it.

the dependence on them is increasing substantially, but food production has not been increasing proportionately even though the area under cultivation is also increasing substantially. Alongwith dam construction, however, the damages caused by floods is not decreasing to any significant extent (see Table 1.3). On the contrary the National Commission on Flood Control estimates that the area ravaged by floods has almost doubled during 1950-80.

TABLE 1.1: Net Irrigated Area by Sources, 1950-79

(in million hectares)

Year	Net Irrigated Area by Sources		
	Canals	Tubewells	Total
1950-51	8.3	NA	20.9
1960-61	10.4	0.13	24.7
1970-71	12.9	4.46	31.1
1978-79	15.0	8.20	38.0

Source: Indian Agriculture in Brief, 18th Edition. Quoted in CSE (1985:112).

TABLE 1.2: Outlay on Development of Irrigational Potential

	Outlay/expenditure (Mil. Rs.)		Cumulative Irrigation Potential (mha)	
	Major & Med. irrign.	Minor irrign.	Major & Med. irrign.	Minor irrign.
Pre-Plan benefits	—	—	9.70	12.90
First Plan	3800*	760	12.20	14.06
Second Plan	3800	1420	14.30	14.79
Third Plan	5810	3280	16.60	17.01
Annual Plan 1966-69	4340	3260	18.10	19.00
Fourth Plan 1969-74	12370 (a)	5130	20.70	23.50
Fifth Plan 1974-78	24420 (b)	6310	24.82	27.30
Annual Plan 1978-79	9770	2370	25.86	28.60
Annual Plan 1979-80	10790	2600	26.60	30.00

Notes: * Inclusive of Rs. 800 million incurred during the pre-planned period.
(a) Excludes plan outlay on unapproved Kaveri-basin.
(b) Excludes non-plan outlay on unapproved Kaveri-basin.
— Figures for minor irrigation pertain to Government outlay.

Source: Sixth Five Year Plan (1980-85), Planning Comm., Government of India. Quoted in CSE (1982 : 60).

TABLE 1.3: Damage caused by Floods During 1953-1981

Year	Cropped Area affected (Lakh hectares)	Total Damage (Million Rupees)	
		At Current Prices	At 1952-53 Prices
1953	9.3	540	520
1954	26.5	580	590
1955	54.0	1190	1340
1956	21.0	510	510
1957	4.5	240	220
1958	14.9	510	460
1959	15.4	790	680
1960	26.5	670	550
1961	18.3	320	260
1962	35.6	930	750
1963	19.7	380	300
1964	24.7	670	450
1965	2.5	60	30
1966	16.1	650	340
1967	33.0	1370	620
1968	26.9	2030	950
1969	43.4	3330	1490
1970	48.5	2870	1210
1971	62.4	6320	2630
1972	24.4	1580	630
1973	76.0	5690	1790
1974	33.0	5690	1400
1975	380.5	4710	1190
1976	76.8	8890	2390
1977	82.5	12000	2820
1978	100.5	14550	3420
1979	20.0	5970	1400
1980	54.1	8300	1950
1981 (as on Aug.19)	16.2	2050	480

Source: CSE (1982 : 62).

Large dams are useful for flood control, navigation, cheap energy, and for perennial and assured irrigation in requisite quantity and at right time resulting in higher gross productivity. Their water is useful for domestic and industrial use. They also have a cooling effect on the local environment and sustain particular varieties of flora and fauna. However, there are significant losses too. A dam across a river creates a huge man-made lake. As a result there is considerable loss of agricultural land, coastal erosion of top soil, forest, wild life and immovable assets of houses, roads, temples, schools and hospitals, archaeological sites and the like. At the same time down-stream there is considerable loss of silt and reduction of soil fertility due to impoundment (Goldsmith and Hildyard, 1984 : 49-60).

In the reservoirs there is considerable loss of water due to evaporation, and transpiration by the aquatic weeds and in the canals due to seepage and also due to over use of water (*ibid* : 61-64).[5] The change in the micro-climate of the area resulting in the moist ecosystem offers ideal conditions for pest infestation and consequently huge loss of agricultural output (*ibid* : 67-71). The change in the micro-climate also directly leads to diseases like malaria, schistosomiaesis, filariasis and river blindness or onchocersiasis. The overcrowding of dam-oustees in poorly facilitated area, bad sanitation and the use of poor quality water also lead to dysentery, gastroenteritis, diarrhoea, hepatitis, cholera and guinea worm. Pneumonia, respiratory infections and tuberculosis are also likely to occur in such over-crowded conditions (*ibid* : 72-88). In the reservoir, lacustrine conditions help in the growth of particular varieties of fishes. There is also loss of fish life in the downstream of a dam and within the sea immediately beyond its estuary (*ibid* : 92-97).[6] The construction of dams in technologically backward countries, in inappropriate places — like seismic prone zones — due to political and cost effective reasons;[7] 'overtapping' during floods; construction on faulty foundations and erroneous design and with inferior materials by unscrupulous contractors; the pilot project syndrome (i.e., the extrapolation of big dams from small dams); sabotage and lack of cooperation among the concerned departments, all usually result in huge loss of life and property due to failure of dams (*ibid* : 103-111).[8] A direct negative result of dam construction is deforestation. The absence of big trees and forests in irrigated area and the compulsive movement of poor people to the upper reaches of the catchment area result in increasing pressure on land and forest and lead to soil erosion and fast silting of the reservoir. Consequently, there is no check in flood havocs because during heavy rains the reservoir cannot store all the water it was expected to (*ibid* : 120-124).[9] Again year-round irrigation from dams leads to water logging, rise in water table, salinisation and loss of productivity in the absence of a proper drainage system (*ibid* : 135-139).[10] There are also considerable problems in managing and maintaining the dam, the power grids and canal network because of huge expenditure, financial bungling, lack of accountability of the bureaucracy, lack of coordination among the concerned departments, apathy of the people and political factors (*ibid* : 167-175). Further perennial irrigation does not simply eradicate poverty in the face of unequal distribution of land. It also leads to polarisation of agrarian classes; puts more emphasis on production of cash crops at the cost of food crops to generate surplus to meet the escalating cost of investment and also to meet the demand of industries (*ibid* : 181-91).[11] Dams are also constructed without giving much thought to the tragedy of population displacement and the problem of resettlement and ecological imbalance. Dams are constructed primarily for political considerations (vote seeking), fattening the contractors and the expectation of 'kickbacks' (*ibid* : 247-257).[12]

The cost-benefit analysis is also heavily biased : it underestimates the costs and overestimates the benefits; usually acts as a foregone conclusion, and in most cases such exercise is done to justify the construction of the dam in question (*ibid* : 265-271).[13] Probably, the worst effect of large dam construction is the social and cultural upheaval. Thousands of people have to shift to some new, sometimes unknown destinations which might be topographically and culturally, vastly different from there own.[14] Revival of their economy and reconstruction of their past social space is a stupendous task. (*ibid* : 27-32). Moreover, resettlement efforts of governments worldwide are dotted with dissatisfaction if not complete failure (*ibid* : 15-16). Despite the obvious benefits of traditional irrigation pattern, the utility of minor irrigation projects and small hydel projects, these are not given due considerations. On the other hand, despite the anticipated man-made tragedy large dam construction will be an ongoing phenomenon in India and the world at large because of politico-economic reasons.

Before the construction of any major dam, the concerned government undertakes a cost-benefit analysis, feasibility study, techno-economic survey, etc. for the particular project. These studies are conducted, not only by government agencies but also by voluntary agencies, autonomous research organisations, and in recent times by major financial bodies like the World Bank and the International Monetary Fund, etc. Most of the investigations and surveys, which sometimes have implicit ideologies behind them, are produced in the form of Reports — typed and cyclostyled — and less frequently in printed forms of books and articles, and hence limited in circulation. Until recent times there was not much published literature regarding the complex process of displacement of and rehabilitation of dam oustees, and much less in India. This is probably because planners and policy-makers the world over, took the evacuees for granted, and assumed that they would move out to new places once they are paid the compensation for their assets. However, the large number of the oustees and the complex problem of their rehabilitation has drawn the attention of international organisations. Hence, these events are increasingly being recorded at least by the civil rights bodies.

In India every year one million people are displaced due to developmental projects, most of whom are tribals (Sarangi and Billorey : 1988 : 829-30). Since the Government of India is championing the cause of the tribals of late, for obvious reasons, the plight of the oustees has come to limelight especially in the media and mostly by civil rights bodies. However, there is very little published literature on them and those are result of collective ventures. It is not our objective to review the available literature one by one but to acquaint the readers with some of the works, which though useful, are not always referred to. Karve and Nimbkar (1969) have studied the people displaced through the Koyna dam in Maharashtra. Even though the report is small in size it is valuable for field researchers. It does not offer, however, a proper framework to analyse oustees of a large scale and complexities. It offers lot of insights regarding the oustees, especially about their problem of assimilation in the new set-up, which is lacking in a recent study by a geographer (Sawant, 1985). The studies by Chandrasekhariah (1965) and Joshi, et al. (1983) fill these gaps to some considerable extent. Both the studies are result of collective effort and are sociological in nature, but different in their approach and emphasis. Joshi, et al. have studied 19 villages in Gujarat which would be affected by the completion of the Narmada Project. These are predominantly tribal villages which were characterized by a fair degree of homogeneity before 1960 but are undergoing differentiation while the construction work is in progress, indicating that the extraneous factor has divisive roles. However, they have emphasised that there is considerable difference both between and within the villages in terms of infrastructural facilities, socio-economic development and social structure and to that extent different villages and different groups within the village are expected to react differently to the condition of displacement and rehabilitation.

Chandrasekhariah has all these problems in mind while talking about the already rehabilitated non-tribal people, of the Tungabhadra Water Spread Area, in different colonies. So the first study is an 'ad hoc' study of predominantly tribal population 'predicting' what would happen to the affected people, whereas the second study is a post-hoc one of essentially caste people suggesting what has gone wrong with the process of displacement and rehabilitation. The first one is more descriptive, rich in ethnographic details and policy oriented. The second one is more quantitative (necessary for comparing the before and after situations), focussed but still bringing out policy implications. Again, the first study emphasises what would happen to individual families or groups of people of a particular tribe/caste whereas the second one emphasises what has happened to the village community in general. Both the studies have devised village typologies befitting their problems and bearing with the methodology. The first study identifies three zones of the sub-merging area classified on the basis of topography, social composition and level of general development. The second one identifies three types of villages — (i) fully affected, (ii) partially affected, and (iii) foreshore villages — depending on the degree of effect of the extraneous factor. These two studies would lead us to believe that in the event of dam construction and the consequent process of displacement and rehabilitation the authorities-that-be are not very sensitive to the social similarities and dissimilarities of the constituents of a village 'community', and to that extent they are thinking mostly in terms of physical rehabilitation of the displaced people. Following from it, the concerned people are undergoing a social crisis. Again, the benefits of the dam have rarely been available to these displaced people. Further, the good intention of the government has been spoilt by vested interest groups, lower bureaucracy, and sometimes lack of co-operation of the concerned people.

These two studies would be very useful for the formulation of our problem. However, since we want to study the effect of dam construction and displacement from a different perspective and in a different context the nature of our inquiries and also the methodology would be different from theirs.

In most recent times there have been several papers relating to the ecological, economic and rehabilitational aspects of various dam projects in India but most of them are available in unpublished forms and are result of collective endeavours, e.g. INTACH, Lokayan,

MARG, NCHSE, NIUA, NPA, PRIA, etc. Most of these were available to us after we had completed a draft of this project.

As regards the construction of large dams, there can be four perspectives from four sections of the population : (a) the government and the bureaucracy; (b) scientists and environmentalists; (c) the people in the catchment area; (d) the people in the command area. It would seem that the government and the bureaucracy always support the construction of dams and go to the extent of constructing them in unsuitable area, primarily for achieving political and economic ends. The bureaucracy, as the mouth-piece of the government, has to support such moves because by doing so they will have 'important' works to perform and enhance the chance of their promotion, perhaps make money in the construction and rehabilitation schemes, and favour their kith and kin in giving jobs and get other benefits from the construction of the dam — compensation, buying new and strategically located land at cheaper price, establishing business, etc.

Scientists and environmentalists might be more objective and go strictly by criteria of feasibility. But while scientists and technocrats are likely to approve of the project from the technical point of view and sometimes also for future promotions and rewards, the environmentalists look further into its social and ecological dimensions and consequently rarely agree to such proposals.

The people in the catchment area, usually in the fertile basins, would hardly want to be dislocated, even if they are poor, because of their unwillingness to start life afresh amid uncertainties. They would not like to be cut off from their kinship/caste/village network especially when they are not the direct beneficiaries of the irrigation scheme (Baboo, 1991(a) : 288-303). The people in the would-be-command area would like the idea because of anticipated agricultural prosperity, year-round employment and demand for certain traditional services. This is not to say that there will be no difference of opinion within a particular group. For instance, within the would-be-command area the land-lords are likely to oppose the move of dam construction because of the anticipated break in their semifeudal nexus in the face of the formal credit system, land legislation, freedom of labour and opening of markets. It is not our objectives here to go into the ethics of dam construction as much to analyse what lessons to derive from the specific case of the Hirakud dam in Orissa. Hence, it is desirable that we discuss in detail about the construction of the Hirakud dam and the specific problems that we are interested in.

NOTES

1. Geographers belonging to the "deterministic" school emphasise that the physical and social conditioning of man is shaped by nature, and man cannot change much against the desire of nature. The "possibilists" emphasise that man can change the physical and social landscape by the application of science and technology.
2. The conservative thinkers usually equate technological development with modernization and westernisation, and consider that in modernizing and modern society there is more and more use of inanimate things. Briefly "Technology is the application of scientific ideas to the environment, providing with the knowledge by which we may be able to make ourselves masters and possessors of nature". See Descartes (1968 : 78) quoted in Michael Redclift, (1984 : 101).
3. In recent times, we have been talking a lot about transfer of technology and appropriate technology in the context of global polarisation in terms of inequality. Especially in the context of underdeveloped or developing countries importing of western technology has been disastrous.

   "Technology is important not simply as the objective of man-made production, but as the mental equipment which translates ideas into action. Far from being apolitical, technology is always political; the means available to a society being structured around social values and interests as well as technical limitation. Once a technology exists its use or non-use implies a political choice". See Eckholm (1976).
4. For a brief reference regarding types of settlement see Scudder (1985 : 125-26).
5. The Percentage of seepage in unlined canals in India amount to 71 per cent at the rate of 15 per cent in canals, 7 per cent in distributaries, 22 per cent in water courses and 27 per cent in field losses. See CSE (1985 : 111).
6. Regarding the decline of fish, Goldsmith and Hildyard observe, "The submerged vegetation and soils soon rot down — thus reducing the amount of available nutrients — whilst competition and predation cuts down the inflated population of those fish species which first dominated the reservoir's ecosystem", (1984 : 92).
7. As regards reservoir induced earthquake David W. Simpson observes, "Since no diagnostic criteria appear to be presently available for determining the risk of triggering induced earthquakes, all large reservoirs must to some extent be considered potential sources of induced activity (1976 : 130). In recent times, Tehri dam, in India, has been very controversial because of possible reservoir-induced seismic activities.
8. Projects like the Tehri in the Himalayas, Idduki and Pooyamkutty in the Western Ghats and Thaubal in the Northeast area have been located in geologically unstable areas. The Koyna dam reservoir caused tremors and earthquake after the impounding of water in 1962. It resulted in killing nearly 200 people, injuring 1500 and rendering thousands of people homeless. Due to bad designing

and poor quality of construction, the Machu dam in Gujarat burst in 1979, killing several hundreds of people, and the Morvi town was destroyed by flood water (CSE, 1982 : 65-66).

9. The resettlement of oustees of the Gumti dam, in the upper catchment area of the Gumti river in Tripura, has accelerated deforestation because of sudden pressure of jhumming by the oustees. Jhumming cultivation on the hill slopes led to further soil erosion (Gupta, 1989 : 2267-70). Unexpected heavy rains in the catchment area of the dams, in the fag end of the rainy season, can create havoc. The Bhakra and Pong dam authorities have been accused of letting out water during heavy rains causing loss of lives and properties (Thukral, 1988 : 4).
10. This has been noted in case of Bhakra command area (CSE, 1985 : 111-12).
11. Choudhri (1987: 23-35) has noted the change in the cropping pattern in the command area of the Tawa dam. Despite the escalating cost and the increase in the area under irrigation, the total production and the yield rate per acre have decreased in this area.
12. In case of mega-projects like the Tehri and the Sardar Sarovar, the immediate beneficiaries are not the oustees as such, but the contractors, their employees and the funders (D'Monte, 1990 : 8).
13. For examples in India see Mankodi (1983) and Paranjpye (1988).
14. The resettlement of Pong dam oustees from Kangra district of Himachal Pradesh in Ganganagar district of Rajasthan, is a case in point (CSE, 1982 : 63). Also see Thukral (1988 : 213).

2

THE HISTORY OF THE HIRAKUD DAM AND THE PROBLEMATIC

Economically Orissa is one of the most backward states in India. This is proved in terms of several indicators of economic development over the last few years.[1] Besides the socio-political factors, natural factors also seem to be responsible for the backwardness. Terrible famines hit Orissa in the 14th, 15th and 16th centuries. In the famine of 1865-66, nearly a million of people perished in the district of Cuttack alone. Since 1868 there have been as many as 39 floods in the Mahanadi Delta (extending over 2300 sq. miles constituting nearly 70 per cent of the Central Delta), the most fertile and densely populated tract in Orissa (Government of India, 1961 : 35). Floods have been almost an annual feature in the three important rivers — Mahanadi, Brahmani and Baitarani in Orissa. There were floods in Orissa in 1834-35, 1845-49, 1852-56, 1911, 1919, 1920, 1925-27, 1929, 1933 and 1937. Common high floods occurred in the three important rivers in 1896, 1960 and 1961. "Common high floods in the Mahanadi-Brahmani delta were experienced in 1896, 1920, 1926, 1934, 1940 and 1955. The years of common high floods in the Brahmani and Baitarani were 1881, 1894, 1907, 1927, 1941 and 1943" (Sinha, 1971 : 71). Though the rivers have fallen almost as rapidly as they rose, the water took a long time to recede from the delta because the drainage of accumulated spills was slow due to flat gradients of the shallow river near the sea, and due to the tidal effects of the latter (Lok Sabha Debate : 13 Sept., 1955). The maximum frequency of the occurrence of floods of all magnitudes was in two phases of the monsoon season, from July 21 to Aug. 7, and from Aug. 21 to Sept. 7. This is the time for transplantation and weeding in the case of paddy and harvesting for 'Biali' (summer paddy). For a cash crop like jute, this is the time for weeding for the second time and harvesting. Hence, these floods cause extensive damage to the standing crops. The damages in terms of loss of human life, cattle and livestock, houses, breaches, sand-cast area, standing crops, and breakdown in communication are enormous. It has not always been evaluated, but on average it amounts to about 12 lakhs rupees (Government of India, 1947 : 49). In 1858, Sir Arthur Cotton of the Commandment Madras Engineers said, "In the last 23 years there have been 3 years of famine, four years of drought, two years of severe inundation, seven years of inundation and seven years of moderate seasons in coastal districts" (Government of Orissa, 1958 : 36).

Such floods and droughts necessarily cause insecurity to life and property; have a demoralising effect on the inhabitants and shatter their enthusiasm to improve ıand, home and village (Agrawal, 1967 : 40-42). During 1911-37, there were nine years of flood with a loss of Rs. 20 to Rs. 66 lakhs on each occasion. The huge loss due to flood topples the gain due to silting of river banks and fields, clearing of the mouth of river from sand and flushing of salt pan created due to perennial irrigation, etc.

There were several Flood Enquiry Committees appointed by the Government of Orissa in 1928, 1938 and 1939-42 to suggest measures to tackle the recommendations for local relief. Floods continued and everytime the same drama was enacted — aerial survey, supply of food, cloth and medicine, dispatching boats and army personnel for rescue operations, etc. by the state and the Centre. After the devastating flood of 1937, Sir M. Visvesvaraya was requested by the Government of Orissa to advise them on the flood control problem. The latter suggested multipurpose water reservoirs, after stressing great need for scientific surveys and continuous observations of the rivers and the delta. The Interim Report of the Orissa Flood Advisory Committee (1938-39 : 6-7) suggested storage reservoirs.

The problem was finally referred to Government of India, in 1945. "The Government of India subsequently passed it on to A.N. Khosla who was the Chairman of the Central Waterways, Irrigation and Navigation Commission. Khosla, after a great deal of study and discussion with the local provincial authorities, came to the conclusion that construction of reservoir was the only cure for many of the problems of Orissa namely floods, droughts, poverty and disease. On the recommendation of Khosla, a conference was held on 8-11-1948 at Cuttack under the chairmanship of the-then Labour Minister B.R. Ambedkar. It was agreed to construct a multipurpose river valley project on the Mahanadi at Hirakud" (*Dist. Stat. Handbook, Sambal-*

pur, 1967 : 398). "In March 1946 the foundation of Hirakud Dam was laid at the site of the dam by the-then Governor of Orissa Sir Harthurun Lewis. The actual construction started in the middle of 1948 and a second foundation of cement concrete work was laid on April 12, 1948 by Jawaharlal Nehru (Sovani and Rath, 1960 : 11). Interestingly, the Khosla Report containing the original schemes and estimates relating to the project were out only in June 1947, but works were already in progress in the mean time. It shows that the construction of such a costly and large dam was a foregone conclusion and it is a matter of conjecture whether the construction work would have been suspended/abandoned if the Technical Reports had suggested otherwise.[2]

Commissioning of Dam

The present dam site was selected after a lot of deliberations. The advantages of the site were : it contains 67 per cent of the drainage area responsible for the floods in the delta; the sub-merged area of the reservoir was exclusively in Orissa; the availability of 'unlimited' quantities of limestone and coal within a radius of 30 miles for the manufacture of cement, an important component; the nearness of Sambalpur railway station and district headquarters; availability of service roads; presence of mineral deposits like iron, manganese, bauxite and limestone in the vicinity for future establishment of ferroalloys, aluminium, cement and other factories; the soundness of the foundation rock and absence of complex geological features;[3] availability of aggregates, sand, suitable earth, and granite stones within the river. These helped in speeding up the work and reducing the cost (Agrawal, 1967 : 21, 40-42; Government of India, 1947 : 17). The small width of the Mahanadi (about two miles) at this point and the presence of two hills on either side — Lum Dungri in the left and Chandli Dungri on the right — leading to lower cost, was also a very important consideration. Further, the 43 affected villages on the right side were hill and forest clad and the rest of the villages on the left side, though fertile, were poorly developed in terms of minerals and roads, and contained no railways, bridges, major structures and hence the loss was assessed to be minimal due to sub-mergence (*ibid* : 27,31). Although the immediate economic cost of the face value of the sub-merged resources were minimal according to official calculation; the long-term and overall cost must be substantial.

People's Protest

The construction of the Hirakud dam came as a part of the post-war reorganisation programme and as an anti-flood measure for the coastal districts of Orissa in the aftermath of the Khosla Report. When it was announced in 1945 a substantial mass agitation, anti-Hirakud dam campaign was launched by the people of Sambalpur district since it was expected to sub-merge 108 full and 141 part revenue villages of Sambalpur district and also 3 full and 33 part villages in Pusar and Saria Police Stations of Madhya Pradesh, respectively. Also the most fertile tract of the Sambalpur district was to sub-merge.[4]

Bharat Nayak, a retired Deputy Collector, opposed the move in 1946 because of unsuitable terrain for laying out canals in Sambalpur; loss of cultivable land and production resulting in movement of population from Sambalpur; emotional problems and prior shortage of labour affecting agriculture. He also suggested alternative ways for flood control and generation of electricity from Duduma water-fall and assessed the loss to Sambalpur district vis-a-vis the gains to coastal districts. On July 12, 1946, he argued that there would be a loss of 15 lakh tons of paddy per annum alongwith loss of mineral resources like diamond, graphite, etc. He also recalled the uproar when a few villages had to be displaced in the Greater Cuttack Plan and the existing problem of unemployment of the local population in the Birla owned Paper Mill at Brajraj Nagar. The main issue was why should Sambalpur suffer for the benefits of the coastal districts; but if necessary the flood affected people could be shifted and rehabilitated. In the last resort, the separation of Sambalpur from the rest of Orissa was their ultimate demand in the meeting of Nov. 10, 1946 which was attended by 30,000 people who demonstrated in front of the Governor of Orissa at Sambalpur. A series of public meetings were organised following the inauguration of the dam, under the leadership of the Gountias of different villages. About 4000 people demonstrated under the leadership of Budhuram Dube, Prahallad Rai Lat, etc., when the PWD Minister visited the dam site. After the first notification served on Sept. 15, 1946 for acquisition of land in 95 villages, processions and meetings were started in Sambalpur. On Nov. 10, 1946, I.P.C. 144 was clamped in Sambalpur and for three months no meetings and processions were allowed in Bargarh and Sadar sub-divisions; 144 was clamped and served on leaders like

Budhuram Dube, Bishnupada Purohit, etc. not to hold/attend any meeting for two months.

Once the demand for separation of Sambalpur from Orissa formed an important basis for the organisation and mobilisation of the people, the local Congress leaders withdrew from the agitation charging it as a conspiracy by the former rulers of the Garjats against democratic planning and development and trying to perpetuate feudal rules, and propagated statements to touch the national sentiments. The move was also disapproved by the State and National Congress including Gandhiji.[5]

The opposition, on the other hand, gathered all possible information including the 26 paged typed technical report of M.G. Rangeya questioning all the rationale offered for the construction of the dam. The movement fizzled out because of the imposing image of the Congress at that time, the arrest of important leaders leading to closure of communication channels, the casual participation of the people especially of the sub-mergible area, the sheer disbelief of people that the rivers like Mahanadi and Ib could ever be dammed, the withdrawal of local Congress leaders and the betrayal of leaders like Budhuram Dube, etc.,[6] and the projection of the dam not merely as an anti-flood measure but as a major developmental project in Orissa in general, and Sambalpur district in particular. It was stressed that Orissa had tremendous wealth in human power which remained unemployed/underemployed; it had water resources which were wasted and it had vast forest and mineral resources which could be exploited with the availability of cheap power and this can be solved through the construction of Hirakud dam. This would facilitate flood control, irrigation, navigation and generation of electricity. Following from it there would be intensive cultivation and incorporation of more land in cultivation, increased productivity and gross production, security against uncertainty and loss in agriculture; new efficient agricultural practices and optimum utilisation of various types of land, crop diversification, labour absorption/more employment, large scale industrialisation, etc. There might also be indirect benefits from social improvement facilities in the form of education, sanitation, medical care, income of State/Centre/people, income tax, postal and railway fare, land revenue and sales tax, water rate, betterment levy, sale proceeds of power, etc. Further it would help in absorbing/moderating flood menace and in preventing erosion of top soil from *aat* and *mal* land and improving the fertility of the soil

(Sovani and Rath, 1960 : 17-18). Even green manures could be grown in fields during May-June.[7]

The Organisation Set-up of the Hirakud Dam

The construction of the dam finally started in the middle of 1948. During the peak period of construction more than 30,000 workers were employed on the project and on an average 25,000 labourers worked for 8 years in it.[8] The machines were worked day and night. The entire area was flood-lit from end to end converting night into day, and all arrangements were made to transport workers to work-site from their colonies and back (Agrawal, 1967 : 36-37, 41-42, 62 & 69; *Times of India*, 1957 : 16). Labourers and skilled workers came from most part of the country. It is estimated that 124 Indian workers out of which 67 were from Orissa, 23 from Madras and 14 from Punjab and two each from Nepal and Pakistan died during the construction of the dam (D.S.H.B., Sambalpur, 1967 : 408).

A new department under the name of 'Hirakud Land Organisation' (hereafter HLO) was set up by the State government for land acquisition, evacuation, compensation, resettlement and rehabilitation of the displaced persons. The duties of the Land Acquisition Officers were to determine the amount of compensation and make payments to displaced persons for their land, houses, trees, etc. An additional LAO dealt with compensation claims for properties acquired for the excavation of the canals. The Land Reclamation Officer, assisted by an Executive Engineer, was responsible for reclaiming the forest area by mechanical operation. The jungle was cleared and the land levelled and marked into agricultural fields. The resettlement staff was responsible for evacuation, and receipt of deposits for land and settlement of people on the reclaimed land. It consisted of a Resettlement Officer, an Agricultural Officer and Medical Officer and assistants.

On Feb. 15, 1947, R.S.Swain, the-then Deputy Commissioner of Sambalpur, made a note (which has been annexed in the Khosla Report: 315-321) regarding the compensation payable for acquiring different kinds of agricultural and non-agricultural land and interests in the sub-merged area which included land, pasturage, houses, temples, wells, schools, tanks, trees, Gountiai interest, etc. He estimated Rs. 5,60,62,635 as the rough cost of acquisition under the project. He anticipated different problems in calculating the compensation, but overall it seems to be a gross underestimation when one takes into account the restructuring of the old assets/facilities after a few years. In fact, by May 30, 1962, the Government of Orissa had paid a compensation of Rs. 8,09,79,032.80 but many cases of arbitration were in the courts yet. A publication of the Ministry of Irrigation and Power (Agrawal, 1967 : 71-77) presents a very rosy picture of "the most orderly evacuation, favourable compensation and habitable rehabilitation". However, the Public Accounts Committee was very critical and observed, "while recognising that in the post-war enthusiasm for multi-purpose project, there was naturally an anxiety to commence and complete such projects with minimum delay, the Sub-committee feel that this did not justify the continued incurring of expenditure on a large scale for an indefinite period of time without following the well-established conventions and rules regarding the execution of works. . . . It is regrettable that the progress of the project is far behind the schedule and must therefore, result in enhanced capital cost, interest charges and delayed returns (Government of India, 1953 : Sixth Report).

The policy recommended in the project report was that "the government should give as compensation, as far as possible, land in exchange for land and house in exchange of house and that too well ahead of the date of actual sub-mergence. The compensation in kind or cash should be on terms which are equitable and if anything generous. The government should assist the people in rehabilitation and strive to create conditions in the colonies which should be a definite improvement on the existing ones " (Khosla Report : X). Model villages with the essential amenities of life, i.e., drinking water, sanitation, schools, community centres, electricity, etc. were suggested. It was also suggested that expenditure on improvements which is in excess of compensation allowance in the project should be met from the General Revenues as a contribution towards the raising standard of living of the people. However, as the Orissa Public Accounts Committee notes, "No comprehensive scheme for reclamation of land was envisaged in the original Project Estimate in 1947 and the estimate did not indicate the cost of reclamation, agency which was to undertake it, the source from which the cost of reclamation was to be met initially and the manner in which the cost of reclamation was to be realised from the resettlers" (Government of Orissa, 1956-57, Vol. III : 110-111). Early in 1949, it was felt that one lakh acres of land should be reclaimed and it was entrusted to the HLO. A scheme for reclaiming 30,000 acres of forest land was sanctioned in 1952. It was expected that by March 1957, 10,000 acres will be fully resettled and the cost of reclamation was to be recovered by sale to settlers at about Rs. 213 per acre. However, due to high cost of reclamation, huge losses, the slow/absence of progress of reclamation and a fall off in number of people desiring resettlement the HLO succeeded in rehabilitating only 10.86 per cent of the total oustees in 4.61 per cent of the total area sub-merged. The policy of giving compensation in cash by the Act of 1948 contributed to the slow down of reclamation work because people preferred to settle in old established villages rather than in the newly reclaimed unknown territory susceptible to the elephant menace.

It may be cited here that there was considerable confusion regarding the jurisdiction of Centre or State Public Accounts Committee over the examination of the account of the project, (Government of Orissa, F.D, Rep. O.P.A.C. 1957-58, Vol. II, 1959 : 52). The Committee thinks that some of the displaced persons may be settled on the fringe of the reservoir beyond the Dykes, who may be given these land for cultivation which will help in resettlement and reduce the problem." They had observed that the higher lands in the reservoir would come out of water by early in the fair season and would become available for cultivation, before the middle of March. Such land to the extent of 35000 acres will be available and will be in keen demand because of deposition of silt and prospects of bumper crops. As it is proposed to maintain the reservoir level below RL 600 up to end of August, even an early kharif crop may be grown on these lands. The tragedy is that the partly affected villagers, who have settled in the periphery of the reservoir have been cultivating such foreshore lease and land lease land in the absence of any afforestation which is leading to the loosening of the soil and silting of the reservoir. Further, the harvest from the fringe land is very uncertain.

Who Benefits

While the gains of the project have been recorded by the Government in the book 'Benefits of the Hirakud Irrigation', the loss in terms of revenue of the sub-merged land, the output from it, forest and produces, grassland, fields, fish, wild-life, spread of peculiar disease from humans/animal and loss of occupation of certain categories (especially of the service castes) of people, etc. have not been properly evaluated. Further, due to demoralisation and psychological set-back there is definitely loss in production. We have already mentioned about the direct and indirect benefits and losses in this project. Further, there are certain general flaws/loss in the construction of this dam:

1. We have mentioned some of these which have not been evaluated properly (including HLO's programme), and to that extent there is under-estimation of cost including the recurring value of forest products, etc. On the other hand, there is over-estimation of benefits.[9]
2. The cost escalation over a period of several years since 1948, in the overall dimensions of the dam and especially regarding maintenance and regeneration have not been properly evaluated. The expenditure in irrigation and electrification, the saving in terms of flood protection and earnings from increased food production and electricity might not justify the construction of such expensive dam.[10] There is a difference between rates charged from individual consumers and industries to the benefit of the capitalists. On the other hand, there is also closure of different industries, due to shortage of electricity due to silting and unimaginative electrification of the rural sector.[11] Again, there is untimely closure of the canals leading to decrease in production of industrial outputs and food crops.[12] It may be mentioned here that despite the increased irrigation facilities in parts of Orissa, the yield of food grains especially during the period 1967-68 and 1983-84 has shown a negative tendency (Gupta, 1989 : 319). Further, navigation in the reservoir, an important objective of the dam, has not materialised due to various reasons.
3. HLO's overall expenditure and the different types of subsidies over years to the dam affected people — rebate of revenue, free supply of manure, partial supply of building materials, ration/grocery items, waiving of loan, etc. — must have been considerable. It can be argued that the government plan should have implemented a proper rehabilitation scheme instead of spending on such non-productive items.[13] People are still not rehabilitated and some people have left the rehabilitated colonies as in Udsung camp. There have also been cases of multiple displacement. There is also fluctuation

in cost-benefit statistics due to unanticipated problems, hurry and oversight. The revised Report of the Hirakud Dam Project of Jan. 1952 showed considerable changes, modification, etc. in the original scheme of 1947. This was not merely due to rise of prices and wages but due to many changes in the Plan Estimates, which changed as the results of the detailed investigations became available. As a result, the lift canal became impracticable and the enhanced cost of Rs. 399 per acre of cultivable area, with regard to the flow canal of 1947, accounted for a truncated canal system.

The difference in project estimates between 1947 and 1952 are summarised as in Table 2.1.

TABLE 2.1: Difference in the Estimates of Hirakud Dam Project: 1947 and 1952

Year	Project Cost in Crores	Gross Command Area in Acres	Cultivable Command Area in Acres	Irrigated Area in Acres
1947	47.81	1.3 lakh	8.6 lakh	1.1 million
1952	89.09	6,43,000	4,52,000	7,91,000

Source: Sovani and Rath (1960 : 8-9).

All these estimates of areas to be irrigated, of power to be generated, crops to be grown, etc. were made without sufficient surveys and investigations, as had been frequently mentioned in the Khosla Report itself. The expectation that hydel power would bring high returns in terms of supply to industries and even to outside state, was belied because of heavy silting leading to decrease in the production of electricity.

4. There is a lack of proper communication among the government departments regarding statistics of compensation, people to be affected, area/villages to be sub-merged, area to be reclaimed and provided, etc. and the flow of information is further suffocated when it is communicated to people. There is lack of inter-departmental organisation, and lack of detailed specification and hence the statistics is subject to manipulation (Viegas, 1991). So, sometimes, people are hoodwinked by it and they become rebellious when the inflated promises are not met with. For example, on August 22, 1983 the then Minis-

> ter of State for Irrigation, Ram Niwas Mirdha, in a written reply in Lok Sabha stated that the original life of the Hirakud Dam was 386 years and the presently assessed one is 147 years (which again is not true); so also the latest construction cost of 67.82 crore rupees is also incorrect.[14]

Even though on June 27, 1946, the then Revenue Divisional Commissioner N. Senapati promised that if any Gountia takes the villagers and goes to another place, he will be given the necessary facilities for building a model village, there was hardly any systematic effort to move and rehabilitate people village wise, which would have given them emotional support to face the difficulties in the initial years. The only way the displaced people could have some identity was by naming the camp/colony after the name of the major/ important village. When people could not be rehabilitated in Government camps many of them preferred to settle in the periphery and sometimes were forced to move when the last date for evacuation came closer. None of the colonies benefited by canal irrigation because the displaced people could not buy costly land in the would-be-irrigated arẹa. The new colonies were located in deforested land and the housing pattern was usually elongated in shape; the planning of the government was not to the liking of the resettlers. There was change in both the quality and the quantity of land bought by the people in the new locality and there were some significant changes in the social relations amongst the new settlers, who necessarily did not come from the same village.

The construction of the Hirakud Dam was completed in 1956. It has a dyke of 13 miles, the main dam is about 3 miles and the maximum height is 195 feet. The construction of the dam has affected 249 villages, 22,144 families, 18,432 houses and 112,038.59 acres of cultivated land which were sub-merged in the Hirakud reservoir (see Appendix-I). The canals have spread over 10 Community Development (C.D.) Blocks in Sambalpur district and 3 C.D. Blocks in Bolangir district. Out of these 13 Blocks, 9 are intensively irrigated and 4 are partly irrigated. In all the Hirakud canal system irrigated 611 villages (partly or wholly) in Sambalpur and Bolangir districts and the gross command are is 3,20,000 acres and 2,20,000 acres in Sambalpur and Bolangir districts respectively (Government of Orissa, 1968 : 178-180; DSHB, 1967 : 402-403).

Once the construction plan of the dam was finalised, people were asked to vacate their native place. People who did not go to settle in the camp, nor went to the periphery of the reservoir chose to stay in/shift to old established villages. The choice of their future habitat depended on several factors. The Brahmins, educated and well-off people very often settled in the towns of Sambalpur, Bargarh, Rengali and Jharsuguda because they could afford to buy costly land or because they were absentee landlords who did not see much prospect in agriculture in the 'new land', especially when they anticipated the shortage of labour (because people would take to construction of own house and reclamation of land), or due to anticipated hardship of camp life or to earn livelihood from urban oriented manual/semi-skilled jobs, to pursue education for children, or to invest in urban estate which they thought would be more remunerative than the rural ones.

People who went to rural area went to live in remote tribal villages or the peasant villages depending on their actual/potential resources to buy agricultural land, to earn from forest or urban labour work or even for the company of friends, relations, acquaintances; the congeniality of the village, facilities of water, availability of cheaper agricultural land and grazing land and house site and the like. Unlike the rehabilitated people in the periphery, these people were not provided with any facility except the provision of potable water and especially if they settled substantially in a chunk. Before we discuss the process of their rehabilitation in detail it is necessary that we spell out the objectives of our study.

The Objectives

Since this is an exploratory study we are not stating the problem in the form of hypotheses but putting them in the form of tentatively formulated questions.

1. *Those who were Evacuated :*

(a) Where did most people like to stay — in the RCs or in other villages/towns? If they further shifted in course of their search for destinations, why did they do so? These people resettled in colonies of different types as well as villages of different spatio-cultural types, i.e., both in irrigated and non-irrigated villages and in tribal, peasant and sub-urban sectors and they shifted in different phases. What factors contributed to their choosing of a particular type of village—their background, different types of social relations with the 'new village' or their assessment of their socio-economic position in the new set up?

(b) Did the government follow any method to choose people to rehabilitate them in the RCs? Who were the people who liked to settle in the RCs? What sort of problems/prospects did they have compared to their earlier situations? Did all of them come from the same or nearby villages? If not, how could they build up relations facing each other as aliens? Did they have to pay the government a part of their compensation money for the facilities made available to them?

(c) In general, were people satisfied with the rate of compensation for land, house, standing crops, trees, etc.? What did people do if they got benefits ultimately? Was there any bureaucratic hurdle to get the amount?

(d) How did people utilise the compensation money? Could they revive their earlier economic position with its help? Did they improve their situation or were they worse off?

(e) How did people, those who did not settle in the RCs, get alongwith their day-to-day activities in the initial period? What was the nature of cooperation and conflict between the new entrants and the old inhabitants of the villages — in terms of food, shelter, land, labour, credit, market and cultural traits like language, attire, behaviour pattern, etc. Has there been any feeling of 'insiders' and 'outsiders'? If the new entrants felt any sense of insecurity or were exploited in any way, what sort of in-built mechanisms did they devise to face the situation? Is there factionalism in these villages based on the notion of 'insiders' and 'outsiders'? Has the relationship changed over a period of time?

(f) Did these 'new entrants' maintain their traditional occupations or did they have to adjust to the new setting according to the factors of demand and supply? What is the nature of social mobility among these people compared to the old inhabitants of the village who came from the same caste, class, ethnic background? Is the social mobility — upward and downward — uniform among the new entrants or there is remarkable difference, and if so what factors account for it?

(g) Did these displaced people undergo any traumatic experience during and after shifting?

2. *The Original Inhabitants of the Village :*

Most of the questions in (e), (f) and (g) above (slightly modified) would be equally applicable from the original inhabitants' point of view because the relationship is always a two way process. Besides, it may be interesting to see how the original inhabitants have undergone socio-economic changes after the arrival of the displaced people.

Further, it would be interesting to see how both the 'new entrants' and the old inhabitants be they in any type of village or R.C. have been affected by the construction of the Dam. Here it would be important to identify factors of change directly following the construction of the dam, e.g., irrigation, electricity, rural industrialisation, urbanisation, more use of extension services, formal legislations, etc.

NOTES

1. In 1977, when there were 18 states in India, the rank of Orissa, according to 43 indicators of economic development, was at the bottom or very close to it. See Government of Orissa (1977 : 195-200). In 1978-79, the per capita income of Orissa (Rs. 860) stood third from the bottom of the all-India average of Rs.1267. See Misra (1984 : 1-3). Further, during the overall period from 1960-61 to 1978-79, the average annual percentage in per capita income between Orissa and all-India was 73.5 per cent. (*ibid* : 4).
2. It should not always be taken for granted that once the foundation stone is laid and work is in progress, a project would be necessarily completed. Public agitation has stalled the irrigation project at Tikkarpara and the Bharat Aluminium Company Limited (BALCO) project at Paikmal in Orissa itself (Dasgupta, 1986). The same was the case with the Silent Valley Project in Kerala.
3. Despite such claims there have been reports to the contrary. See S.N.Qn.8(a) government attention to Blitz, Dec. 12, 1953 "Crack in 30 Crore Hirakud Dam" which speaks of defective framework, and improper grouting of underneath rock. Recently there have been reports regarding use of inferior construction material at the Narmada Project.
4. This figure from Hirakud Dam Circle Office does not tally with the figures in *District Statistical Hand Book, Sambalpur*, 1967 : 407. Further the number of expected sub-merged villages has changed from time to time. (Supakar, 1988 : 10).
5. For this part I have drawn heavily from the paper 'The Hirakud Rehabilitation and the Displaced People' by Prasanna K. Tripathy and Sukadeva Nanda submitted to *Seminar on Development and Displacement*, Institute for Study of Society and Culture, Burla, December 20-21, 1987, who themselves have com-

piled it from the reports of *Samaj* daily published during 1946-1957.

6. It is alleged that Budhuram Dube, an important leader of the anti-Hirakud Dam movement, remained cool, and pacified the agitators after accepting a monthly salary of Rs. 1000 to act as a government pleader. People told that he died after prolonged illness and lot of sufferings only because he let down the people and was indirectly the cause of their sufferings.
7. It is beyond our scope to prove and evaluate these expected benefits. But looking back some other benefits seem to have occurred, e.g., paddy plants are now being nurtured and made ready for transplantation, in late summer, by irrigating it with stored water in pool, tank, etc. There are more water in all the reservoirs of the district because of year-round passage of water from the dam. Development of transport and communication — as in the case of N.H. 6 connecting Calcutta to Bombay through Sambalpur and connecting of Sambalpur to Titlagarh by rail — could be made possible after the bridge over river Mahanadi in 1950-51.
8. "The stone-cutters came from the South, blacksmiths, carpenters, welders, etc. came from the Punjab and engineers and supervisory staff originated from, apart from these two, several other states . . . the local worker constituted 70 per cent of the total number of unskilled workers. Majority of them are from Ganjam district and the neighbouring areas; a good number of them came also from Bilaspur district in M.P. . . . Wages at Hirakud have been good. The unskilled workers get Rs. 1 to 8 per day; the women Re. 1, the skilled worker gets Rs. 60 p.m. For higher skilled workers the wage rate is up to Rs. 180 p.m." See "Mobilising an Army of Workers for the Hirakud Project", Hirakud Dam Supplement, *The Times of India*, Jan. 13, 1957. p. 16.
9. Besides unforeseen contingent factors such as earthquake and unseasonal heavy rain leading to the collapse of the dam and the huge loss of life and property, which usually is not a part of the benefit-cost analysis, there is usually excessive expectation of gains and underestimation of cost, especially of the rehabilitational aspects. See for instance, Kashyap Mankodi (1983).
10. For a succint analysis of this nature see Vijay Paranjpye, (1988).
11. Tracing the regular seasonal power crisis in Orissa to over-dependence on hydel power of Hirakud, Balimela and Machkund a staff correspondent writes, "Thoughtless expansion of the rural electricity network has virtually become a mockery, particularly in the wake of the current power shortage. While urban centres continue to grapple with inadequate and restricted supply of power, electrified rural centres plunge in prolonged darkness. Lift irrigation points and agricultural pumpsets remain idle. Rice-hullers and agro-based cottage industries, however small their numbers be, also remain unproductive on powerless days". See "Orissa facing acute power crisis", *The Times of India*, April 4, 1983, p. 6. For data regarding higher rate of annual siltation in selected reservoirs, see *Report of the Irrigation Commission* quoted in CSE (1982 : 62).
12. Besides the usual closure for repairing, for which it is pre-notified, the Hirakud canal system is very often closed at a time when the farmers are in utmost need of water because due to silting the reservoir has a false storage capacity and there has to be minimum water in the dam for production of electricity to maintain essential things function. Such closure leads to loss of agricultural produces and hence loss in industries, also. Besides, there are several varieties

of pests developing in the irrigated belt of Sambalpur district for which the farmers and the Agricultural Extension Officer (AEO) have no answer. On the face of steep increase in the price of pesticides the loss to farmers is significant.

13. As the saying goes prevention is better than cure. Robert Chambers (1970 : 253) goes on to suggest that compensation may be paid in productive assets, such as boats and nets for fisherman, and tools, seeds and roads for farmers. Also see Mankodi (1986).
14. For example, see:
    (a) Lok Sabha Debate, 22.8.83, 'Construction cost of major dams'.
    (b) Lok Sabha Debate, 13.11.62, 'Statement correcting the reply given on 30th May, 1962 to S.Q.No.1182 regarding Hirakud Project regarding compensation amount paid so far'.

3

THE FIELD OF STUDY AND THE TECHNIQUES OF DATA COLLECTION

I chose to study the after-effects of Hirakud Dam rather than any other dam in India, or to study an on-going project, such as the Rengali dam in Orissa, or the Sardar Sarovar in Gujarat which has been very much in the news in recent times, because of the following reasons: (i) I wanted to learn from the past and suggest measures for the future. (ii) It is probably the only major dam in India which has displaced the least percentage of tribals (18.34) compared to caste groups. While tribals do not necessarily survive on agriculture and do not stick to jajmani ties, caste groups do, and to that extent the caste groups are likely to suffer more if they are displaced from an area booming with agricultural activities as happened in the case of Hirakud dam. (iii) Observation of on-going phenomena of this nature, which sometimes take decades together for completion, is difficult by a single researcher as in my case, and that too within two years period, and hence I chose to study a completed project. (iv) Sovani and Rath (1960) had emphasised that all the secondary and tertiary benefits of the Hirakud dam should be visible after 25-30 years from the date of its construction and hence I considered it an opportune moment to study. Even though their's is not a sociological study, it served as a bench mark regarding economic aspects. (v) This was one of the earliest major dams in Independent India and had generated lot of expectations in the post-war reorganisation period. Neither the policy-makers/implementing-authorities nor the affected people had much experience about the things to follow; was more of an experimental situation and hence the case is likely to be more complex and interesting. (vi) Finally, I had the acquaintance with the area and the language which usually ease up the burden of field work.

The construction of the Hirakud dam in 1956 across the rivers Mahanadi and Ib in Orissa sub-merged 249 villages (108 fully and 141 partly) in Sambalpur district of Orissa and 36 villages (3 fully and 33 partly) in Pusar and Saria Police Stations of Madhya Pradesh. The affected people, who had different degrees of contact with the native and neighbouring villagers, left the villages completely or partly depending on several structural conditions. Some of them went to settle in the resettlement camps/colonies,[1] and in some cases, later moved to other localities or vice-versa. Some others settled just on the periphery of the reservoir and thereby lived in their earlier villages (which were partly sub-merged) or in a new locality very much in the vicinity of the earlier village. Some of them also moved into old established villages of different spatio-cultural categories. To make the study fairly representative I selected two colonies and eight villages from four different settings. The four settings were : (i) a colony which is the transplantation of a whole sub-merged village, i.e., a homogeneous colony, (ii) a colony which is the transplantation of a few (small and fragmented) villages, i.e., a heterogeneous colony, (iii) two foreshore villages one of which is partly sub-merged and the other is completely sub-merged but resettled very close to the earlier one, (iv) six villages of different spatio-cultural categories — tribal dry village (TDV), tribal wet village (TWV), peasant dry village (PDV), peasant wet village (PWV), sub-urban dry village (SDV), sub-urban wet village (SWV) — where there were at least twenty households of the oustees in each of the pre-existing villages. To get rid of problems regarding distance, geographical variation, etc. and to have cultural continuity, I selected all the localities in Sambalpur district of Orissa, which has been most affected by the construction of the Hirakud dam.

The rationale behind this scheme is that : in the first setting we can study households who knew each other but are now interacting in a new ecology and have new opportunity structures, provided mostly by the State. The population is fairly 'homogeneous'. In the second setting one group of people interact with another group/other group(s) of people who are virtually unknown to each other, and live again in a new ecology and under new opportunities. The population is 'heterogeneous' compared to the first setting. In the third setting we have households who might or might not have lost their land and houses. They are now living nearer to a vast reservoir of water and have missed their links with the nearby villagers. In the fourth setting a few households of oustees interact with villagers of an existing village (not necessarily in a new ecology) where they are maintaining on their own resources. The oustees are usually a minority in such a situation and have an underdog image.

The population of these four different settings — of disturbed and relatively undisturbed categories — have been affected differently by the construction of the dam and the follow-up actions. This framework would help us in understanding peoples' rationale behind selection of settlement vis-a-vis the various formal/informal opportunities, which might ultimately help in the formulation of rehabilitational policy measures.

A census study was conducted for all the displaced households in the concerned colonies, the two peripheral/foreshore villages and the six villages of the fourth setting. I had thought of comparing equal number of households, as that of the oustees, from the original village by stratified random sampling method but this was not possible because the original inhabitants in all places have a social status different from the oustees.[2] Hence, I had to talk to reliable key informants of the comparable categories to draw conclusions regarding socio-economic mobility (both upward and downward) of the oustees.

Data for this study were collected from both primary and secondary sources. The secondary sources were published material relating to dams in general, and Hirakud dam in particular. Publications of the Central Water and Power Commission, Bureau of Statistics and Economics of the Government of Orissa, Records at the Collectorate of Sambalpur and the Hirakud Dam Circle Office were very useful. However, collection of data from these sources were very cumbersome and sometimes frustrating because the records were brittle, those were not systematically arranged and not maintained properly. Moreover, the office assistants, who were actually dealing with the concerned files have retired; the Hirakud Land Organisation has even been wound up and the present office assistants are not very much acquainted with those files. It is rather surprising that even when all the affected persons have not received their due compensation the officials have become casual towards record keeping. Further, the government officers were usually not very keen on tracing the old records which were dumped in dark and dusty rooms. The clerks and peons were least interested to help which would not give them some informal booty. The fixed office hours, holidays and the distance of the formal organisations and the offices, from the field, delayed the work.

The primary data included the responses of the displaced population, the original inhabitants of the villages, officers of the-then times who were in charge of evacuation and resettlement and the activists who had participated in the protest movements against the construction of the dam. Data from the respondents and informants were collected mostly with the help of an interview guide.[3] Besides informal interviews data were also collected by quasi-participant observation, group interviews and case studies.

It was not really very easy to select the localities because they were scattered in different parts of Sambalpur district. Initially it was difficult to get a list of the villages which were partly or fully submerged, the nature of their movement to new localities, a list of the camps and colonies, and their further movement form the first place of resettlement. I had to 'beat around the bush', contact people on my own who were expected to be in a position to provide some clues or information, which were not always true or helpful, and visit villages/colonies which did not very often suit my requirements. After the initial running around it was possible to trace the final locales with the information provided by the oustees themselves. To get rid of several biases in the selection of the locales I had defined the categories clearly. The colonies/villages should have, at least, 80 households, the tribal villages should be near the forests, have at least 70 per cent of Scheduled Tribe population and preferably from not more than two tribes; other villages should be multi-caste; at least 70 per cent of the land should be canal irrigated to be called an irrigated (wet) village; the sub-urban village should be within two km. of a town and have minimum urban amenities, and the peasant villages should not be near the forest. In actual practice, however, certain practical aspects had to be considered, e.g., accommodation, food, transport and overall congenial environment for field work. These factors were, however, inconsequential most of the time. For initial entry into the field, I never took help of any official because their introduction of the researcher very often alienates the researcher from a sizeable population in the field and the researcher is very often considered as a government agent/development worker and the like, and hence there is suppression and exaggeration of information.

After finalising the interview guide, selecting the localities and collecting the basic information from the District Record Room regarding the landholding of the villagers, I started my actual field work in February 1987. I started with the first setting, which was a complete transplantation of one sub-merged village in a resettlement colony. My idea was to move from simple to complex social structure, to have verifiable authentic information from people who have undergone almost similar experience and to be in a position to infer the nature of changes of the same group of people during last 40 years or so. From this homogenous situation I gradually moved onto heterogeneous situation, i.e., to the second, third and the fourth setting respectively. Depending on the size, complexity, degree of cooperation from the locality and the respondents, I spent 15 days to one month in a locality and completed the field work in 8 months, in two different phases, i.e., February – May 1987 and September – December 1987. After writing the first draft I wanted to go to the field once more to collect certain basic information from government offices, to cross-check some information and to interview some more senior people who were either activists or witness to the resistance movement connected with the Hirakud dam. This was not possible because of paucity of time. I would have liked to complete the field work at a stretch but this was not possible because of some difficulties. This break resulted in loss of valuable time, extra-expenditure and indifferent health. The point that I am emphasising is that such intensive field work should be completed at a stretch. People those who have the experience of the difference of general life styles in remote villages of India, as in Orissa, and that in Delhi, would appreciate my point.

Even though the localities were part of the same district with some sort of cultural similarities, those were different in terms of the problem of rehabilitation of the oustees; more over the modes of earning livelihood were different. Hence I had to use different techniques to study different localities. While conducting the research I had to keep several things in mind : my own social background, sociability and temperament; my specific roles; the expectations of the respondents and their anxieties; the section to be started with; the time, place and overall environment of the observations and interviews; particular time of the year especially with regard to agricultural season/economic activities/social functions; practical difficulties of collecting data from both formal organisations and informal groups or individuals; the sensitivity of the problem under investigation, and the nature of questions at a particular point of time; preparation of genealogical chart for the inhabitants of the localities; factions in those localities; and continuous learning from field techniques and to be in a position not to displease any individual or sections of the localities.

Four out of the six villages in the fourth setting were already known to me during an earlier research conducted seven years ago. So there was not much problem for arranging for food and stay there, and this was probably possible because of my past 'good' behaviour. I stayed and ate at the same place that I had been doing last time except in one place because the earlier host had expired in the mean time. In rest of the localities there were initial problems of arranging the basic necessities; some times people who had consented to provide for these things on payment backed out when I reached there with my luggages. Sometimes people hesitated to provide food because of my higher caste background and then looked at me differently when I took my food from S.Cs and S.Ts. Over years of field work experience I have come to believe that people, these days, are not taking the researcher for granted. They are increasingly suspicious about his identity and purpose. Further, they do not want to waste their time and reveal information to objective/value-neutral researcher who can not be of any help to them in material life. 'What is the meaning and utility of this work', they usually ask.

My stay at Delhi aroused a lot of interest in them and they kept on inquiring about the city life and about the Sahebs and the Ministers. Most of the time they cooperated with me because they were considerably impressed by my concern for them despite my higher caste/class background and educational attainment. My origin from a village (and my knowledge of the local dialect) also enabled me to interact with them more freely. My keen interests in their day-to-day activities, their past and their immediate problems endeared me to them and sometimes they asked me to be present in their decisive meetings and cultural functions. Sometimes, they asked me to write applications to the concerned authorities for repairing of the village tanks, roads and sheds or school building, for financial helps from different agencies, etc.

They expected that my research should convince the government to take suitable measures to ameliorate their economic conditions. The influential ones sometimes entertained me at their homes; tried to conceal their oppressive/exploitative designs and suggested me to write things in such a way that they would benefit more from the developmental activities. In all the cases I never told the villagers that my research is going to solve their major problems, but I had assured them that I will write the 'truth' and if it attracts the attention of the government. I would feel satisfied. I was sure that assuring them of something, which is not under my control, would land me in difficulties if I have to restudy them later on.

During the fieldwork, I always started with the have-nots with the assumptions that these people have nothing to lose by telling the truth. They were always very cooperative also which I had confirmed during my earlier visits to field. However, I never tried to displease the influential/rich sections who were very often the employers/patrons of the poor. Further, I had to be very cautious about factions in the villages, which is a part of life in rural Sambalpur. Sometimes, factions helped me in collecting very sensitive information from the opposite faction and sometimes in verifying the information, which of course requires lot of tact and caution.

Since I was concerned basically with agrarian population and mostly with people of low means, I went to interview people when they were not very busy with any economic activity. I also saw to it that the respondents are in a position to express their views and make their statements without any inhibition. Hence people with conflicting interests were not interviewed in face-to-face situations. People with common interests were sometimes interviewed in groups to see if they had disagreements. I wanted to write, as little as possible in front of people because they were afraid 'to go on record'; but beacause of the limitations of time and memory I often combined the activities of interviewing, noting, and observing their facial behaviour. While interviewing people in groups if some body from the 'opposition camp' happened to reach there, which happens very often in small localities, then people quarreled among themselves and I had a tough time to tackle them. Sometimes I had to depend solely on the key informants to verify such conflicting views. Government Records sometimes helped in such verification also. While interviewing people at home, the women folk, especially of the would-be-well off families, become very suspicious when the questions pertain to earnings/income and expenditure. Poor people very often go on describing their miseries and become very emotional especially when it comes to matters such as death, disease, accidents and economic ruins. Sometimes I found it very difficult to control myself in such situations but I was still in a position to console them and to be in a position to record the responses. From such experiences, I can very well see the impropriety of the questionnaire/schedule method for collecting data from such groups. When most of the people in this district are having a marginal existence, it pained me very often to disturb them in field or at home when they are relaxing after hard work for whom I was not in a position to provide any compensation.

I wanted to do the field work at such time of the year that the agrarian population were not very busy in their economic activities but since I had to conduct the work round the year, it was not possible to avoid the peak ploughing, transplanting and harvesting seasons. Availability of electricity in some localities enabled me to work faster, whereas its non-availability delayed the work. Sometimes observance of some social/cultural functions facilitated me to work faster because most of the people were available around. Sometimes extreme weather (especially rain and heat) and peak agricultural activities delayed the work.

As regards the localities, the people in the dry area were more cooperative than people in the wet area; within a particular area the poor were more cooperative than the rich. Sometimes there were no members in some families who were witness to the displacement and rehabilitation operations. Hence we had to infer their conditions from the reports given by their relatives or fellow villagers. There were also very old people whose statements and opinions would have been very useful, but sometimes they were not in a position to speak or listen. It was more so in the case of the displaced who had undergone a lot of difficulties. It was also reported that many of them died earlier than expected because they had to work very hard in the initial years after displacement. Many of them kept on thinking of their bygone days and hence suffered from psychological setback. Sometimes the young and the old ones differed very much in their opinions regarding displacement and rehabilitation which was noted during group interview and also at domestic situations. At such stage, we had to take a very balanced position to avoid distortions. The final place of resettlement was crucial for the people, and the people who took the final decision were to be blamed or praised depending on the present conditions of the concerned people. This was the cause of dissatisfaction in some localities and had led to factions in some villages. This placed me sometimes in embarrassing position.

For each locality I always prepared a genealogical chart and had the 'Record of Rights' regarding land which enabled me to be more familiar with the respondents. But since the localities were scattered, because of their diverse characteristics, and I kept on moving from place to place, it was difficult sometimes to figure out respondents when I met them in market places or in towns. However, I did not have any real problem confronting such situations.

Given the sensitivity of the topic, the limitation of time, the problems of arranging food, stay and other basic necessities especially for someone used to the urban facilities, the rather nomadic movement from place to place of diverse settings, the convulsion between objective inquiry and research ethics as well as social responsibility for a people who have lost the rhythm of their life, I had tough time collecting data from people to write their epitaph. The respondents did not always take me for granted and asked a lot of embarrassing questions in the initial phase : they did not believe that the information will be used as knowledge because during the initial phase of dam construction the concerned officials had collected information from them which was later used to oust them from their native locales. Notwithstanding all these difficulties, I had to go on slowly but steadily as I moved from one locale to the other being richer in experience and learning things to counter the fresh difficulties. There was one major problem : I had not read any published/unpublished literature regarding the social aspects of the Hirakud dam, nor I had heard much about it before the field work. So sometimes I had not been in a position to cross-question, nor in a position to throw searching questions, which could be overcome after I covered the first setting. A general idea about the topography, agriculture, cultural traits and economic opportunities would have helped me to face the respondents more confidently. There is one more important problem; it was generally observed that people do depend too much on government and outside agencies for improving their lot; they do not think more in terms of collective initiative. Hence, they had a tendency to inflate their difficulties and spoke a lot against the corruptions among politicians and bureaucrats, accused them for their present wretched conditions, and kept on pressing me to write about their difficulties. I wish I have been able to distinguish the objective situations from the subjective ones.

NOTES

1. A camp is a temporary rehabilitation centre for people needing emergency shelter whereas a resettlement colony usually refers to a permanent shelter for displaced people. However, these two terms have been used interchangeably in

this work because the word camp is more frequently used by people but which essentially refers to the colony.

2. This is not to suggest that migrants/refugees/foreigners/outsiders always have an underdog position when they enter a new locality.
3. The interview guide was pre-tested during a pilot survey during October-November 1986, when I moved from village to village and colony to colony in search of the actual locales I have ultimately selected.

4

REHABILITATION OF THE OUSTEES IN RESETTLEMENT COLONIES : The Homogeneous Vs. The Heterogeneous Setting

Introduction

In this section we will be concerned with the process of resettlement of two colonies, which took place during the fag end of the construction of the Hirakud dam. The most important difference between these two colonies is that, as far as the social composition goes, one colony consists almost exclusively of people of one fully sub-merged village, whereas the second colony has population from both partly and fully sub-merged villages and hence has a heterogeneous population. A comparison of the two colonies before the sub-mergence is not possible even though the villages or parts of the villages, which form part of the two colonies, were situated in the same Katarbaga Police station and sometimes had similar topography, cropping pattern and cultural profile.

This task is all the more difficult because it was not possible to portray a composite picture of the villages which later constituted the heterogenous colony because of the non-availability of reliable data and non-availability/difficulty in collecting data for all these villages. Further, we could not lay hands on any material depicting the condition of people of the would-be-sub-merging villages of the 1950s. Hence it would be useful, rather desirable, to discuss the two localities one-by-one and then compare them at the end. But before we do so, we would like to mention the processes of land acquisition, compensation, displacement and rehabilitation which were sometimes common to all the localities. We are doing so to avoid repetition in subsequent chapters.

When officials came for measurement of houses, land and enquired about different assets to be sub-merged, people in many villages did not cooperate. Since the villagers were panic-stricken and disturbed in the whole exercise in the initial phase, and in some areas there were resistance movements, the officers were not allowed to measure the houses and no information was given to them. Consequently, the officials had a tough time in noting things.

When people enquired about the motive behind those activities, the officers did not clarify the issues but simply told that they would come to know later. People necessarily became suspicious because large scale survey work was undertaken by Indian and foreign officials regarding the River Level (RL), the area to be sub-merged, etc. The officers stayed in the camps on hillocks and had very little interaction with the villagers. Despite all these, people in some villages, did cooperate with the officers. Some of the clever people of these villages demanded more compensation by bribing the officers and or influencing the latter. They did so by inflating the measurement and type of materials used in the house. People who had some idea about the functioning of the bureaucracy took to different types of malpractices to get more compensation for land, house, trees and other assets. The malpractices included recent renovation of house to claim for a new one, claiming some dead/absentee's house, changing the classification of land, etc.

During 1948-56, people were served Notice under rule 4 and 5 and thereby told that they were entitled to get so much of compensation for their land, house, trees and permanent structures like pond, tank, temple, etc. In case they had objection or if there was any error in Notice 5, they could complain within 7 days failing which the government's decision would be binding on them. The government usually paid compensation at the rate of 500 times the annual assessment of revenue on any piece of land. For house the size, type of materials, and the duration after construction were taken into account. Usually nobody was given less than Rs. 100 for a house. Regarding trees the variety, size and life span was taken into account.

Sometimes there was some error here and there in the Notice, under rule 5, and people had to go all the way to Sambalpur to collect cheque even for eight *annas* (fifty paise). The Chowkidar and the Jhankar were asked to be alert those days to avert thefts because all the villagers had received compensation. The villagers also cooperated in the night. Many people had not seen so much amount of money in their life time. Many of them did not know counting of the currency notes because they were used to coins. People were afraid of the notes getting drenched, burnt, mutilated, eaten up/destroyed by mites, mouse or the like. Since most people were used to keep coins underground, in earthen pots or in the hole of trees, there were instances of people losing money in this way. Sometimes poor/illiterate and innocent people were also cheated of their money and it was all they had for their tangible assets; once it was gone they became virtually destitutes. Sometimes people received compensation for one portion of their total land or house and spent the money in litigation to claim more amount for the rest of their assets and in the process became virtually paupers at least temporarily. It was also reported that when the village was partly sub-merged there were different problems. Only the sub-merged portions were compensated. If a man had part of his land above RL 632, he did not get any compensation for that part of the land. So he had to sell off that portion, forget about it, or cultivate it while staying in some other colony or village. People who wanted to leave such partly sub-merged village had to demolish their house before taking compensation for it, on the suspicion that they might stay back there after getting the compensation. Hence, when some people came back to the partly sub-merged village after finding it difficult to adjust elsewhere, could not occupy their own house/house-site. It was rather a folly on the part of the government not to use such deserted houses for rehabilitation of the left over poor in the village.

People of the Kulta caste, in most of the villages, invariably deposited all/most of the compensation amount immediately in the village with the concerned officers and hence were in a position to get the best land in the resettlement colony, which was being distributed according to first-come-first-served basis. The lower castes and labourers, who did not always own land, and whose primary occupation was not agriculture, spent their little compensation on house, little amount of land (if at all) and on errands. They spent on buying gold, silver, utensils, bicycles, clothes especially of silk and tusser, eating and drinking and treating/entertaining friends and relatives (sometimes of the unaffected area) who were too happy to be there because their relatives had got 'windfall' money. The vendors, of these items, virtually camped in these villages during the payment of compensation and until a few days later. Clever people gave them shelter and food in lieu of a remuneration. It is told that women from lower castes/classes and tribals became yellow after putting on gold ornaments because gold was available for Rs. 60 per *tola* and silver was available for Re.0.50 per *tola*. It was also reported that people purchased bicycles not for any business but for pleasure trips. Many people loaned out money to their persuasive/needy relatives and never got them back and hence had strained relationship later on. Some people also consulted specialist doctors, quacks and wizards to get rid of diseases from which they were suffering for a long time, but could not consult them earlier for lack of money. Many people also went to pilgrimage, which is usually the life time ambition of people in the villages.

Once money was received by people, they were sure that they have to move sooner or later. Then came the Notice No. 5 which informed that they have to shift to some new resettlement colonies or to the destination of their choice latest by such and such date. The date was fixed keeping in view the flooding of the reservoir, convenience of the government officials, and of agricultural operations, suitable month of the year (to avoid rainy season), availability of conveyance given that it was a large scale operation, and the convenience/inconvenience of the evacuees. However, the preparedness of the evacuees was the last priority. A household was allowed only one trip of free transport by truck; more than one household were allotted one trip if they did not have much belongings. Sometimes influential people and Gountias/Zamindars were allowed more than one trip; the excess trips were to be paid for. Rich people having huge stock of paddy, etc. shifted the same over weeks/months by bullock carts/trucks. People were usually allowed to take rice, paddy, household goods, and wooden huller in one truck, they were not allowed to carry window/door-sills, roofing materials, logs, bricks and stones, sugarcane crushers, etc. in that truck. People with insufficient/medium resources used their/hired bullock carts to transport these before/after their actual shifting by truck. Many of them first left their family members in the new locality and did the shifting gradually. Since people had to shift within a limited time span (before the rainy season, and before the village became deserted), and there was little chance of mutual cooperation among the substantial owners, people had to incur expenditure on transportation and undergo lot of difficulties; productive activities came to a grinding halt. Family members, if all of them were going to one destination or even kinsmen and villagers, did help to the best extent possible but since the destination was not always nearer hiring of transport service was necessary. When convenient, people transported the goods by boats also, otherwise by road. If they were coming down stream then things were transported by rafts, also.

When people moved to 'unknown' localities, they kept their household goods, paddy, etc., with some friends, relatives or newly made acquaintances or volunteers in the village until they constructed their own houses in the village. During this interim period sometimes the hosts behaved very nicely with them and did not tamper with their belongings. Since, even until the last hour before shifting, many people had not decided about their final destination — and even now some people are still in the process of shifting from one locality to another — they kept their belongings temporarily with such people. As a result there were many cases of misappropriation of money, paddy, rice, consumable goods and even utensils and jewellery leading to strained relations, quarrel, litigation and pauperisation of the evacuees.

When evacuees went to *surua gan* (old established villages) usually they had some relatives, relatives'/own friends, and acquaintances there — through prior contract, through business, trade routes, suitable location in terms of one's own calling. Sometimes people went to a village because some other people of their village were going there who had prior connection. If the incoming population were not too much for the existing facilities in the village, then the evacuees did not have much problem in terms of physical amenities — water, housing, open space, etc. and they did not have to bother for it. Those facilities had to be personally/collectively arranged or provided for by the government in the new resettlement colonies. To the extent that certain facilities cannot individually be arranged, e.g., tank, the evacuees had to depend on the government or tried collectively if possible; but if they came from different villages and were unknown to each other such joint effort was difficult to come by.

In the new villages the guests were very often provided with shelter, food, fodder and social protection varying from a few days to a few years depending on the closeness of relationship with the host. Sometimes, close relatives housed the evacuees and arranged to purchase land for them; sold part of theirs in nominal price or allowed them to cultivate land free or on lease which very often led to bitter relations when the grown-up children of the host felt deprived or could not tolerate the prosperity of the 'guests'. Sometimes such help was extended because due to provision of canal irrigation, intensive cultivation, and land reclamation, etc., the hosts needed labour power, which was provided by the evacuees. In some villages the evacuees were welcomed if they happened to be from the service castes like washerman, barber, etc., and if there were no corresponding castes with regard to the demand. On the other hand, they were not encouraged to settle in some villages if they were considered as potential/actual competitors in scarce resources like agricultural land, pasture, firewood, water, etc. Rich/influential people of the village, who were waiting for the right opportunity to buy land at lower prices from the poor, distressed and the absentee/extravagant Gountia/Zamindar, etc. created uncongenial situations for the incoming evacuees. Initially they dissuaded them from coming there saying that theirs' was a notorious village or that there were many witches or that some people were suffering from leprosy and incurable diseases, etc. Where the evacuees managed to enter such village because of some pull factors, the 'trouble makers' made their life miserable by physical threats; disgraced them in public; prohibited them directly or indirectly from enjoying public facilities; impounded their cattle on the ground of trespassing, and damage of crops. They forcibly collected subscription for socio-religious functions, did not allow them to take water from public wells on the ground of doubtful caste; did not allow them to construct the face of their house towards theirs on some pretexts; pelted stones at their houses and treated them as outsiders.

Once the vehicles, provided by the government came to the villages, people panicked even though they were already notified. Some people collapsed on the spot; sometimes ailing people, expectant ladies, and old ones had lot of problems. It was really painful to leave home and the hearth for ever for an uncertain future. Some people could not shift everything they wanted to. The contractors and the drivers of the truck had to think in terms of their own profit also; they allowed limited time. People had to hurry up; even if the food was ready they could not take it. If they asked to stop the vehicle on the way the driver did not oblige. Sometimes the driver left them stranded half-way and treated the evacuees very badly; at times there were altercations also but people generally acted as underdogs.[3]

Often the vehicles did not come as scheduled and people kept on waiting throughout the day and were put to lot of inconvenience since they had already dismantled everything. When people had to move things in parts, the family members had to be divided at two places. People from the neighbouring village (if they did not shift) and the host village sometimes made a fortune in transporting the belongings of the oustees. Because of dense jungle and the threats from tigers, very often people had to move in groups while transporting their things in bullock-carts. This required some coordination. When the oustees left the village, people from the Pahilpar (on the other side of the river) came and stole away the sized stones, earthen tiles and other building materials; standing crops and fruits, those had been left behind, and the trees on the fields which were very often transported across the river.

The shifting was organised in two phases during 1955-56. In the first year people very close to the river banks were asked to shift since these villages would be immediately affected by flooding the reservoir/bridging the river and closing the shutters. But the gates were not closed that year. Shifting started after the harvest of paddy in January until June.[4] So some people, even after getting compensation and shifting to the new locality, came back temporarily for cultivation and reaped the crops. This was envied upon by government officers and people of pre-settled villages.

(A) Re-Constructing Social Structure: The Case of a Resettlement Colony of a Transplanted Village

Village Kudopali with an area of 275.17 acres and a population of 275 in 1951, was situated on the West bank of river Ib. It was surrounded by river and rivulets in such a way that people found it difficult to move out in rainy season, especially if there was flood.[5] Besides, there were five ponds and one tank. That is water was abundantly available. The village was elongated in shape; the Brahmin Gountia stayed at one end of the village and the ward where the Gandas stayed was at the other extreme end. People of other castes resided block by block. Kulla was the biggest village around having Brahmin as the dominant caste, who usually did not perform the agricultural operations themselves. Hence, people from Kudopali leased in land and also worked for the Brahmins of Kulla. The village did not have the service castes like blacksmith, barber, washerman, and sweeper/scavenger (Ghasia) and depended on the nearby villages for their services. There were just two petty shops in the village. So the villagers went to the nearby weekly markets for sale/purchase and borrowed from the Marwaris of Kulla and Rengali.

The classification of the land had this pattern : grazing and village forest — 8.09 acres, settlements and roads — 10.89 acres, sub-merged — 16.93 acres, garden — 0.25 acre, illegal cultivation — 0.95 acre, and rest 239.01 acres in the possession of the tenants. The terrain was plain and the soil had good water holding capacity. The fields could retain water for a long time and were less susceptible to drought. People did not have to toil hard for raising crops.

The major crops of the village were paddy (mostly broadcast), gram, sugarcane, bhang, castor, horse gram, onion, white peas and wheat. Because of the fertile soil and easy availability of water round the year people could practise mixed cropping and could grow more than two crops in a year. The village was so prosperous that for revenue assessment it was considered as 100 units. The productivity of paddy from different types of land, per acre, in qtl., was : bottom land — 14, del — 9.5, and upland I — 7.5.

The village was famous for its paddy, gram, sugarcane, brinjal as well as for its hospitality and performance of religious activities. There was no shortage of labour especially because people grew varieties of paddy — with different maturing period and in different types of land — and had mutual exchange of labour and livestock. The villagers respected the Gountia and provided informal obligatory labour. The jajmani system was also very strong. The condition of the labourers was very satisfactory because payment was made in kind and the attached labourers — mostly Gouds and Gandas — got a small share in every thing produced by the employer. The casual labourers received payment in kind according to the nature of activities, such as ploughing, weeding, thinning, transplanting, etc. The attached labourers usually received 35 kg. to 47 kg. of paddy per month as wage and 3.74 qtl. to 4.68 qtl. of paddy per annum as annual attachment. Besides they received several considerations, advance payment, and overtime remuneration. People usually bought kerosene, salt, cloths and cattle from weekly markets, which they exchanged for kinds, very often. People of this village were famous for cattle trading for which they went to the markets at Bargarh, Sambalpur, Padiabahal, Bhukta, Sargipali, and even up to Sakti and Champa in Madhya Pradesh.[6] The Gountias and the Marwaris lent out money for this trade and the individual trader could make a profit of Rs. 500 to Rs. 700 per season those days.

In the old village the Brahmins and the Kultas did well in agriculture and trade. The Keuts and the Majhians managed well on fishing and making of parched rice. The Gandaś pulled on weaving and agricultural labour and the Gauds managed with agriculture, labour, herding and milk. So even though land was very skewedly distributed, all of them survived and prospered and nobody starved. The villagers had a strong collective feeling which was sustained and furthered by the performance of religious functions and festivities.

The villagers acted as a cohesive unit. Minor differences were always resolved in the village by the Gountia with the help of old people of respective castes, or by the caste panchayats. In their living memory people had not witnessed any general crisis leading to change in inter-personal or inter-group relationship.[7]

The people of this village and that of the area, in general, had a very strong feeling against the people on the other side of the river Mahanadi, because that side traditionally suffered from poor soil resulting in poverty and starvation; it was also infamous for litigation and theft.[8]

Such feeling was so strong that the old people had warned the younger ones that in the event of any crisis also they should not go to reside in the Pahilpar. When news about the construction of the Hirakud dam came in 1946, it reached the villagers from Kulla and other weekly markets. It was discussed widely in Kulla and Mura. But the villagers did not believe it at all. They said, "when we are unable to close a break in our field-embankment during flood, how come the government be able to bridge permanently the two major rivers Mahanadi and Ib". They took it as a canard. However, when the first notice came, telling that they have to vacate their native place latest by 1956 in lieu of suitable compensation by the government, they felt the real pinch. People gathered on their courtyards and discussed the matter; everybody guessed something or the other and tried to communicate the latest rumour/information that he had heard from the nearby village/town/market-place. People kept on discussing as to where to go, what to do, how to resettle in a new locality, what would happen to their property, and the relationship with their kinsmen who live in the nearby territory. They were not sure whether the government would rehabilitate them providing land and house or they had to do everything on their own; how much compensation they would get and whether it would be enough for their economic rehabilitation, etc. Such mental tensions had their adverse impact on productive activities. The villagers were not certain as to when they would have to shift, if at all. Long maturing crop like sugarcane suffered and people did not take any interest in improving their land, fencing their gardens and repairing their houses thinking it to be non-economic ventures and also because they were disheartened. During this uncertain phase, the villagers had joined the resistance movement against the construction of the Hirakud dam. The villagers had provided at least one person from each household and had been twice to Sambalpur for demonstration; even ladies had participated. The demonstration was peaceful; there was no compulsion to participate in it and there was no collection of cash or kinds for any fund to sustain the movement.

In the mean time government officials provided conveyance to the villagers to see different would-be-camp sites. Some of these sites were being forest-cleared and others still covered with dense forests. The villagers sent some of their representatives to visit the sites. The Gountia did not go to see this site because he wanted to go to stay with a relative in some old established village but he had assured his consent to collective decision. The villagers were not satisfied with any site because they were not used to forest land and apprehended damage of crops by wild elephants. Moreover, there was hardly any good source of water. They wanted to shift enblock and hence availability of required amount of land was also another important factor. The government had promised them all basic amenities, reclaimed land and housing materials but they were very sceptic. They had chosen the Basupali area but the government did not allow them to settle there because people from several other villages had also chosen that site. So ultimately they selected a locality where people of their neighbouring villages also chose to resettle nearby and also because if was just five km. away from the old Ranchi Road. the locality was also close to a cluster of big old villages with school, hospital and weekly markets. They thought that in times of crisis they could depend on these big villages for employment and could take to trading because it was linked with Sambalpur by road. However, the decision was taken primarily by the Kultas and the Gauds and others followed suit with the idea that when they die in the new place they would die together. The small size of the village and the collective feeling made it possible. The Brahmins and the Gandas were very indecisive because the former can not do agricultural operations by themselves without the help of the Ganda labourers. But the Gandas had little land and could not hope for enough land with their anticipated meagre compensation and thought of unemployment in the absence of the Brahmins. The Majhians and the Keuts — who depended mostly on fishing — had little stake in the negotiation. They watched the situation.

The colony has been named after the old village Kudopali. It is situated about 25 km. North West of Sambalpur, 5 km. from Parmanpur and the nearest pitch road; and 5 km. from the biggest colony Mura with a High School and the Police Station. A bus plies twice from Mura to Sambalpur via this colony and there are quite a few connections from Parmanpur. So it is well-connected compared to the old village, as regards transport. The PACS at Rasiapali is 2 km. away. The Regional Rural Bank (RRB) at Sason is 15 km. away, and the Land Development Bank (LDB) and the State Bank of India, Agricultural Development Bank (SBI, ADB) are at Sambalpur. The nearest Post office is at Mura. The village was just one ward, now it has two wards.

People of Kudopali wanted to shift in late summer (May) but the government asked them to shift in January. People who came in the first year, came within 15 days' duration. Unfortunately, that year there was unseasonal winter rains over 10 days. Some people had already dismantled the roofing materials for shifting, while waiting for the trucks, but due to rains and muddy roads trucks could not come for a few days and these people had to seek shelter in others' houses who did not shift that year or who had not dismantled their roofs. One Kulta household came here one year in advance when government officials started the operations of land reclamation, construction of roads and digging of tank Nos. 1 and 2. During this time some people went on constructing their houses on some demarketed plots, phase by phase, and shifted next year. Most of the people came straight without any preparation. Initially they stayed for a few days in the government constructed/provided huts made of clay, straw and *daro* (dried and straight branches). It was extremely hot that year and it was more painful to people who were living on the bank of the river. People had to sleep on hard-baked earth because they kept their household goods on cots to protect those from termites; cooked food had to be hung on rope-work (*sika*) to protect it from dog, cat and other animals because there was no proper door in the house/hut. People were very afraid of snakes, which roamed around in abundance, after their natural abodes were cleared. Since all the jungles were not cleared at a stretch people had also to be cautious of wild animals, and the cattle had to be driven back home well before sun set. Because of scarcity of space at home the cattle had to stand under the shady trees during hot summer. There was acute scarcity of water also, even though there were tanks, because in the very first year the tanks collapsed when fast streams from the jungle entered the tanks. Inside the village the roads were full of stubbles of trees and people found it difficult to walk on them. When people came here the land was being reclaimed slowly by chopper machines and bulldozers. When rain was about to set in people demanded land and hence the contractors asked the workers to hurry up. As a result a lot of stubbles of big trees were left on the fields. Forest land were necessarily undulating with several streams and hence the land could not be levelled properly. Further, fields were identified and demarketed by thin embankments and the terrain was slanting. So in the very first rains many embankments were washed away. Since people had been just shown their plots and there were no clear demarkation of fields by stone poles, people got confused. Because the final *pattas* were handed over to the tenants after 10 years, some of them had not known their fields properly; it led to litigations also. Since the fields were full of stones, stubbles and other unwanted things the owners took many years to clear those things. There were many pits which were partly covered with these things alongwith dried branches and leaves. When rain set in, these things caved in an people could not fill them because many fields were already sown with paddy. People were not sure, very often, as to what variety of paddy to sow because the seeds they were used to could not necessarily fit in the jungle soil. People had to work very hard for first ten years to make their land produce good crops. All these works could not be done by family labour alone, especially when they had to struggle against several unknown and hitherto unacquainted forces. So the Kisan and the Khadia tribals from nearby villages were engaged in such land reclamation works. People who did not have sufficient money or could not spare it for some reason, had to toil very hard to make their land productive. The government gave Rs. 20 per acre of land for this purpose but that was insufficient. Men and bullocks got injured while ploughing the land because of the stone and stubbles in them and all of them were affected by jungle mosquitoes, which could be warded off sometimes by smoke. The soil did not have water absorbing capacity since the clay was loose, being mixed with sand and pebbles, and hence water got drained off hours after heavy rain. So the paddy plants could not be thinned out as is done to weed out the undesirable plants, because the roots of the paddy plants would hang in that case. People had to eat rice, which had not gone through the requisite process, and it was difficult to digest. Transplantation method was also rarely possible because most of the land were not suitable for it. Moreover, there were not many suitable plots to raise seedlings. However, people who got bottom land could harvest reasonable crops for the first two years because water could be stored in these plots and it was rich with organic ingredients in the form of dried leaves and shrubs which went down at the time of levelling the ground. But the overall yield for these households and for the rest of the villagers was just hopeless. Most of the people were not in a position to recover their seeds, even.

Before shifting many people had sold part of their livestock, especially draught animals, because of anticipated scarcity of fodder and pasture in the colony. On top of it lot of the cattle died in the colony because they were bitten by jungle mosquitoes. They could not get the long grass that they were used to eat near the rivers; they drank the dirty stored water of the jungle streams (rotten with dried leaves) and had to simply survive on leaves. Initially the bullocks, while grazing, went back to the old village, and had to be searched for leading to wastage of time. Sometimes, they were stolen and way-laid by neighbouring villagers who considered the arrival of the oustees as encroachment on their natural resources such as jungle fruits, pasture, firewood, etc. The overall loss of cattle and low (sometimes negative) yield meant poverty for the people. Many people had goats and the place was very suitable for raising them, but those had to be sold out gradually to meet expenditure during their pauperisation.

In the first year only Kultas and Gouds came to this colony who had immediately deposited their money in the old village after getting the compensation and necessarily got the best land below tank Nos. 1 and 2. House sites were allotted to them by the Camp Officers; the area was 0.04 acre for house and 0.08 acre for kitchen gardens. The colony was planned in a rectangular shape with wide roads and lanes. The exact location of the house was left to the choice of evacuees. The Brahmins who came here in the second year, stayed in the centre of the colony; the Kultas and the Gandas on either extreme ends of the colony, and rest of the castes/tribe used the remaining space. But the Keuts were requested to stay in such a way that each ward had close excess to a Keut's house for getting parched rice.[9]

The vacant space in between blocks was there to avoid catching of fire and that is why the houses were not located in compact groups as is the pattern in old established villages. People of the Kudopali colony did not like (and more so in Kashipali) such barriers and many of the lanes have been encroached for housing or for the purpose of kitchen gardens. This shows that even if the planning of the government was a novel device from the point of safety and hygiene, people have their own likings and dislikings and sometimes with logic. The separation/isolation of houses and the wide roads are helpful for thieves. The wide roads are desirable for transport and the drains were provided for drainage, especially of rain water. However, the roads and half-filled drains are rarely maintained by the inhabitants of the colony. In fact most of the housewives sweep the front portion of their houses and dump the garbage in the middle of the road. It looks very ugly (and stinks in rainy season), as in Kudopali and Kashipali they do not have any weekly sweeper (Ghasia). This shows that people do not maintain properly the facilities provided by the government and keep on depending on the government for their maintenance and renovations, etc.

Land, in this colony, were allotted to people on first-deposit first-preference basis. So all the Kultas got the best land in the colony, which are now irrigated from tank Nos. 1 and 2, and they grow summer paddy (*dalua*) also. The Gouds were supposed to get similar land since they had deposited money in the old village. But the Gountia who came one year late to this colony persuaded the Revenue Officers to transfer part of it to his name. The officers obliged and the Gouds, who were the 'disciples' of the Gountia and who were afraid of him as well, consented to this proposal by getting inferior land in exchange. This was possible on paper because the final *patta* had not been issued until then. The irrigated land mentioned in Table 4.1 against the castes other than Kulta are not situated below tanks No. 1 and 2, but below two small ponds which mostly irrigate the land of the Brahmins in the season crop nd partly help in vegetable gardening but very rarely they retain water in summer. It is also alleged that a chunk of ten acres of land that is below these small ponds were supposed to be allotted to the potters (Kumbhar) but again the Gountia played tricks to have it in his name. When people were not allotted the plots they were shown, or did not get the amount of land they were assured to get, they were told that their money fell short of the

TABLE 4.1: Distribution of Resources in the Homogeneous Resettlement Colony

Castes/ Tribes	No. of h.h	% to the total	Total popln.	% to the total	Amt. of land (in acres) 1926	Amt. of total land (in acres) 1987	Amt. of land irrigated (in acres) 1987	% of irrigated to total land	Amt. of land per h.h. (in acres)	Bullocks in pairs	Amt. of land per pair of bullocks (in acres)
Brahmin	12	14.12	67	16.54	73.65	92.67	17.43	18.81	7.72	4	23.17
Kulta	38	44.71	163	40.25	127.49	181.67	59.43	32.71	4.78	34	5.34
Goud	8	9.41	33	8.15	11.67	19.66	2.38	12.11	2.46	7	2.81
Teli	1	1.18	7	1.73	0	0	0	0	—	1	—
Kumbhar	5	5.88	31	7.65	0	12.54	0.72	5.74	2.51	3	4.18
Keut	4	4.71	25	6.17	0	13.20	2.13	16.14	3.30	4	3.30
Majhian	0	0	0	0	0.31	2.70	0	0	—	0	—
Ganda	16	18.82	70	17.28	16.57	19.85	0.25	1.26	1.24	5	3.97
Bhuyan	1	1.18	9	2.22	7.85	6.77	0	0	6.77	1	6.77
Munda	0	0	0	0	1.34	0	0	0	—	0	—
Total	85	100.01	405	99.99	238.88	349.06	82.34	23.59	4.11	59	5.92

Sources: 1. Personal Field study.
2. The amount of land, for all the localities in this study, correspond to the Record of Rights of the tenants of the concerned localities of different settlements.

Notes: The ratio of land to bullocks does not explain anything in terms of zero and one (e.g., 0/1 or 1/0). In such case we connote it by '—'.

amount required for the area and that the rest of the amount could be collected back from Sambalpur. The implication is that there were enough opportunities for manipulation in the allotment of land and that influential and rich/clever people could bribe/persuade the officers to get the chunk of land that they desired, if they paid the required money. Since land is a tangible asset and crucial in agrarian economy people did not hesitate to violate collective norms to serve selfish ends. It is gathered that the camp/settlement officers did not want to break the old political order — the reign of the Gountia — (and thereby invite trouble) in the new colony; persuaded the Gountias to stay there so that there headache about rehabilitation would be over and there would not be indiscipline among the tenants. Hence, they conceded to many of their (sometimes unreasonable) demands and pampered them. That is *status quo* of the old place was maintained in the new colony despite the changes in several arenas.

In the very first year tank No. 1 collapsed at one point during rainy season. As a result one big plot of land of a Kulta got sandcast but he did not receive any help from the government for reclamation. The sluices in the tanks have been made in the middle and the sides. The side ones are meant for releasing the surplus water, especially in the rainy season; the middle ones are meant for irrigation during scarcity but those have been placed at such depth that once they are completely opened they can drain the tanks empty. Since the Kultas are raising long maturing paddy (*bad dhan*) for higher yield, they drain out more water in the season crop so that there is little water for the summer crop and hence again they are the only people close to the tanks to raise summer paddy. If there would have been more water in the tanks and if the sluices in the middle, would have been located a little up then more people could grow vegetables, groundnut, sugarcane and pulses, etc.

The Kultas' greed and selfishness is condemned by the lower castes and even by the Brahmins. Excess release of water from the tanks in rainy season means scarcity even during October, when others required water to irrigate their paddy fields at the tail end, resulting in substantial loss. The Brahmin Gountia is also responsible for this since more water in tank No. 2 means the sub-mergence of part of his land above this tank. So he does not protest the Kultas' releasing more water through the middle sluice, which is also useful to him for his land below tank No. 2. Since cultivation of paddy is less labour intensive compared to vegetables which require continuous attention, marketing, etc. the Kultas are more interested in paddy. The moist land below the tanks cannot raise anything except paddy because it is usually water logged due to seepage of water in land right below the tanks. But to cultivate paddy, and that too of long maturing variety, and thereby deprive others from producing a second crop is harmful to others. The Gandas and others, who do not have irrigated land at all, are naturally envious of the Kultas who cultivate a second crop of paddy and who employ the Gandas occasionally in labour work. Since the Kultas live on one extreme end of the village on one side of the temple, the rest of the villagers always refer to 'this' or 'that' side of the temple. That is there is a clear cut physical and economic distantiation between the Kultas and the rest of the population or at least between the Kultas and the Gandas.

When people came to settle in the Kudopali colony, many of them initially stayed in the huts provided by the government and we have already mentioned their difficulties. After the unbearable summer it rained heavily and all the huts collapsed that year. But by that time most of the people had already constructed partly/fully temporary houses. The present houses in the village have been constructed mostly after 1975 when people could revive their economy to some extent. Except the Gandas most of them have earthen tiles-thatched house, which is a symbol of some prosperity in this area. The Gandas lived for the present and constructed straw-thatched houses, which of course requires annual repairing. Since they were mostly wage earners, neither had they got the money nor the time to construct the costly and durable tile-thatched houses with timber/logs. Others could construct good houses because of non-availability of straw in the initial years, when there was little production of paddy (and the bullocks had also to be give straw as fodder), cheap and easy availability of timber and bamboo from the nearby forest and the cheap availability of earthen tiles and their own resources to meet the labour supply. The government officers had also encouraged them to use the timber available around telling that they would not have to pay for it, but later some people have been charged minimally for these material. People had to spend substantially for land reclamation and construction of houses and for most people the compensation paid for their houses, in the old village, was not enough to construct similar house in the new colony. In the old village also many of them had good tile-thatched houses and the Gandas had straw-thatched houses. Given a golden opportunity also the Gandas could not benefit because of their own inertia as much for the lack of their initial resources. The Kultas always stress on good house, good bullock and good land because they are down-to-earth cultivators. This is not to suggest the economic development or under-development of people of a caste purely in terms of its cultural traits but as far as our present area is concerned, it has to be an important criterion alongwith other objective factors, as we will see later.

In the initial years the Commissioner, HLO, and the other officials connected with it visited the colony on request to inspect certain on-going activities like construction of roads, tanks, wells, school and temple, etc. and to settle disputes also. Kudopali is part of a huge resettlement colony complex of Nua-Mura. There was a plan to inter-connect the tanks in this complex for regulating the level of water and also for equitable distribution of water. This was essentially a novel idea but it did not succeed/materialise due to lack of coordination among government officials and the people of the colony, and also because of lack of official initiative to construct canals, sluices, etc. Even today this would be a good idea to start afresh so that the whole area can be irrigated at least for the season crop, if not for the summer crop. And it would be befitting because the oustees, who sacrificed so much for the construction of the Hirakud dam, would benefit.

As reported by the people in Kudopali colony many of the promises of the government, such as the provision of all the permanent structures in the colony as there were in the old village, or equivalent compensation, have never been fulfilled. The concerned officials had told them that they would not have to pay land revenue for 20 years. However, after 10 years of stay they were asked to pay the revenue and that too retrospectively. People underwent a lot of difficulties since they had suffered repeated loss from agriculture. They had also to pay for the logs/timber they had used for housing. They were also assured of a hospital which functioned much later after repeated representation by people of the colony complex and is situated at Mura, five km. away. As regards the help of the government people remember land reclamation grant of Rs. 20 per acre and *tacavi* loan; the latter was extracted back from the people but it was waived in the year 1980. By then all the people of this colony had repaid the overdues. The loans from the PACS at Rasiapali, which started financing since 1962, was not of much help in the sense that people who did not have the irrigated land were not in a position to repay the loan. People depicted the story of over-charging, harassment, seizure of household goods, etc. for default. They also remember the supply of controlled rice, wheat and the free dole of ghee and atta during *Nabanna* and *Pousa Purnima*, in the first two years, and the recent (after 1980) distribution of CARE feeding to the kids in the colony.

We have already mentioned that people encountered a lot of difficulties regarding potable water, shelter and means of livelihood in the initial years. In the first year most of them consumed their stock of paddy in sowing and eating. The landless lower castes had already exhausted their stock by the beginning of the monsoon because they could not go to earn their wage when they spent their time in construction of the house and reclamation of their land. During the rainy season (and it rained very heavily that year) they could not go out for wage. There was not much agricultural operation to be done also because people simply ploughed their fields and sowed the paddy seeds as the rains set in and individual owners went on reconstructing the embankments of their fields. After the rainy season construction work in tank No. 7, at Mura, started and most of the people went to work there as casual and contract labourers. The distance of the site from the colony is 7 km. People went there to work in the morning and came back in the evening. The wage, as is even today, was not attractive but people had to work to earn minimum for the sustenance of the family. Expectant mothers, women with small kids, and the old people who could not go to work engaged themselves in collection of firewood, house-keeping and paddy husking. In the second year when the rest of the villagers came to the colony, the Brahmins kept four attached labourers and a few casual labourers from the Keut, the Goud and the Ganda castes. The Brahmins also employed casual labourers for the construction of their houses. Nobody in the colony employed labourers for agricultural operations since people were in a position to manage their work with family labour and exchange labour. They did not have saving to pay the wage, also.

The agricultural history of this colony from 1957 to 1971 is a tragic one. It is dotted by low rainfall, drought leading to near-famine condition, pest due to excessive rain and the like. During these difficult years people lost their 'dignity', did the type of works that they had never done in their life and survived on jungle fruits (mango, palm, date, *bel*, *char*, *mahua*, etc.), roots (*kasur*, *dhulu*, etc.), leaves (bamboo, tamarind, *kachher*, *mamer*, *sunsunia*, etc.) and mushrooms.

Initially they hesitated a lot to tell their humiliating experience but later confided in me in telling unbelievable and heart-rending experiences (stories). "Among hard things we have not eaten stone and among soft/liquid things we have not eaten human stool. We have taken rest of the things", they told. They competed among themselves and amongst animals for these eatables. It was reported, with lot of anguish, by an up-coming Kulta that once he was attacked by a bear while waiting under a palm tree for the palm to fall in windy weather. Others told about many accidents and escape from the grip of snakes, bears and boars, etc. while looking out for such food; three of them were bitten by jackal and one of them died, also.

During this period of crisis 34 people from this colony went out to spray DDT for a period of 4 months in a year. These people gave part of the DDT powder, meant for spary, to individual household and got some rice, oil, salt, vegetables, etc. in exchange. Then once in a week/fortnight somebody would come back to the colony and give some money to the concerned households and enquire about their inconveniences, etc. and communicate back the messages to his fellow workers. It was told that once, while going to a village in the jungle, they were chased by a wild tusker; they survived by hiding themselves inside a pipe, under a bridge, meant for draining water. They used to come back to the colony during rainy season for agricultural operations.

When there was no gainful labour work available in and around the colony, the Gandas collected firewood/timbers from the nearby jungles (which is virtually extinct now) and sold those in the nearby irrigated villages and were in a position to earn an amount equivalent to the daily wage. People from other castes took to petty trading in rice, vegetables, fish, chicken, bamboo-shoots, bamboo baskets, etc. They also sold the forest produce they had collected. Petty-trading in rice was the most important activity. People bought second-hand bicycles by arranging some money or loan and went to buy paddy from double-cropped villages as far as Lachida and Patrapali at a distance of 70 km. They went in groups of five, at least. Because of uneven/muddy roads, they anticipated problems: somebody might fall down, somebody's tube might get punctured (and there might not be any repairing shop nearby), somebody might faint on the way due to distance and load. At a time one could bring 75 to 100 kg. of paddy. Then one had to buy/collect firewood, perboil the paddy, dehull it by *dhenki*, clean it and again take it to the nearby villages/markets for selling. Both men and women were involved in this occupation. It was reported that scores of bamboo mattress (*talei*) would be found at a time along the village roads for containing/drying the perboiled paddy and that women had to tie rags to their feet to get rid of swelling in their feet while dehusking paddy. After 1965 people took the dried perboiled paddy to rice-hullers at Parmanpur and later to Vikampur and since 1980 in the colony itself, to get it dehulled. This saved them from some physical drudgery, but the males and females had to wait quite some time to get their paddy dehulled; sometimes failure of electricity furthered their problem.[10]

People have left trading in cattle since 1956 but there is still one Kulta who goes to the cattle market at Bargarh by bus 80 km. away, and walks back to the villages/colony alongwith the newly purchased bullocks for somebody by taking a remuneration of Rs. 60 per pair of bullocks. There are some Kultas, even now in this colony, who buy bullocks from distant markets at cheaper prices, nurture them properly for a year or two and then sell in nearby double-cropped villages for a much higher price. During the crisis in agriculture not only paddy production was at its beneath, but straw also. Insufficient straw and non-availability of long grass affected the cattle. The Gandas who used to borrow and buy a few bundles of straw had to buy those from outside at a much higher price for thatching their houses. People were compelled to sell their good bullocks in higher prices and buy cheaper ones just to manage their cultivation. During the scarcity it was difficult to pay the herdsboy (*nariha*) and that is why also people sold the bullocks. At Kudopali colony almost all the households have at least one pair of bullocks, with most of them not costing more than Rs. 500 per pair, whereas a good pair of bullocks cost around Rs. 3000 in this locality. Most of the Kultas have such good bullocks.

One remunerative and important activity, which is available to all the people, irrespective of caste and sex, is bidi making. In the old village nobody knew it because they did not have kendu leaves nearby and there was no agent or contractor for arranging it. First a few women of this colony went to the nearby colony where there were a few women engaged in this occupation and learnt it over a few months. They, in turn, taught it to people in their own colony. There are two agents within the colony and one from a nearby colony who provide kendu leaves, bhang and thread to the people. A grown-up male/female can make up to 1500 bidi along with minor domestic works and earn a wage of Rs. 12 at the maximum. The old people who were busy with taking to urgent domestic/economic activities and could not take initiative in learning this could not learn it later on. It was reported by them that because grown-up boys and girls made bidis together, there were cases of their elopement in some other colonies/neighbouring villages.

Table 4.1 shows that only 24 per cent of the land is irrigated from all sources. In practice, however, most of the 'irrigated' land of the Kultas, 2.00 acres land of the Brahmin Gountia and 2.46 acres land of the Gouds grow a second crop of paddy and rest of it is assured of irrigation in season crop if there is normal rainfall and/or if the tanks are filled up. About 15 per cent of the land of the colony has never borne any crop and the people have been trying their best to cultivate rest of the fallow land if these plots are situated near any source of water including streams of the jungle. During agricultural crisis due to low yield, lack of surplus and lack of absorption of labourers in the colony, most of the people lived hand-to-mouth. They went to work in agricultural operations and other works such as construction and earth works, in the neighbouring villages and colonies. After the introduction of a second summer crop of paddy in these localities, these people managed to find jobs round the year and did so if they were physically fit. While going for work the whole colony looked deserted; only the old, infirm and the children were left behind. Big children nursed the small ones, lactating mothers squeezed milk from their breast and kept it for the babies. Hence, children rarely went to the Lower Primary School which later became a Upper Primary School. The paddy received as wage was boiled and dehusked at home to have rice. In this way there was hardly any leisure for the people and hence they could not take to religio-cultural functions they were doing earlier; they did not have the resources to do so also.

During this period people who had borrowed from the PACS and the Revenue Office could not repay it and were harassed in several ways. The loan was not written off; the Revenue Deptt. also collected revenue arrears. Many people had to pawn their gold and silver ornaments and utensils to get some money initially from the Gountia, and the Marwaris at Vikampur and Rengali. Almost all of them forfeited the collaterals. The lower caste people who had purchased intangible items, after getting the compensation, were the worst sufferers.

It is reported that after 15 years of land reclamation and cultivation, the cultivable land of the colony started giving some good yield and it was further helped by irrigation from the tanks. When people saw the second crop of paddy being harvested by people in the nearby colonies of Rasiapali and Mura, they also started growing the summer paddy. In the first two years people were very hesitant and cautious and cultivated it only on a part of their irrigated land because they would not have been in a position to withstand further major loss. At that time the cost of production was not much in terms of water tax, labour charge and fertilizers. There was not much of pest infestation either. So the Kultas were in a position to revive their economy substantially. They also took to market gardening in the uplands near the government laid canals. The people also started growing groundnut after getting this idea by the people of Mura. The growing of groundnut was not confined to Kultas alone but to almost all the people. The Gandas were again the worst sufferers in this regard. The Gandas' land do not have any source of water and the land is also rocky; so it is not suitable for growing groundnut. Further, it lies in one extreme periphery of the colony and hence susceptible to damage by jackals, deers, and boars. Only one Ganda household has only 0.25 acre of irrigated land, which is not suitable for the summer paddy. He had bought this piece of land from a Kulta widow and grows groundnut, onion, garlic, tomato, water-melon, etc. He is the most prosperous amongst the Gandas. There is virtually a class-caste congruence in this colony.

We have already seen the occupational diversification of people during the agricultural crisis. The Brahmins have been leasing out part of their land to the Kultas and the Gouds since they did not do the agricultural operations on their own, nor did they have sufficient resources to employ attached labourers round the year. They also did not take to petty trading in different wares and labour activities of different sorts. Seven of the twelve households have taken to education and are in white-collar jobs such as lecturer, teacher, supervisor, Village Level Workers (V.L.W.), Police Officer, etc. One of them is a professional cook and does priestly work and there is another man who is a reputed priest in this area. Besides, most of the women members know bidi making. Three of the households stay most of the time out of the colony to pursue their jobs; others commute. In the old village they would never have taken to bidi making or to parched rice even for consumption in the family, not to talk of selling it through somebody. The brother of the Gountia worked as Kendu leaf supervisor (*munsi*) for a small sum for a long time, and goes to nearby weekly markets with a tailoring machine for stitching clothes. He could not have imagined of such a work in the old village. Now that the children of the Gountia household are already having higher education and they have land in strategic position, and have connection in the job market, they are expected to revive their old status gradually. However, the expenditure involved in marrying off their grown-up daughters might unsettle them economically, at least temporarily.

The Kultas have almost revived their economic status since they own irrigated land in strategic position and have taken to several enterprising activities by cutting down the consumption to the minimum. The Gouds are gradually coming up by agriculture, blue-collar work, petty trading and rearing of goats. The Kumbhars (potters) and the Keuts (fishermen/parched rice-makers) are taking to their traditional jobs. The Kumbhars are gradually improving their situation because of demands from the nearby irrigated villages but they are facing a lot of difficulties regarding clay, firewood, straw, and facing competition from substitute machine-made items. The Majhians are not staying in this colony because they could not survive on agriculture, and preferred fishing in the reservoir. Now their houses are dilapidated or completely extinct since they have been living on fishing in the periphery of the Hirakud reservoir and come to the colony only during festivities and religious functions. The Bhuyans are living on agriculture and salary of two school teachers in the family. Besides, they have a little income from priestly duties also. Most of the Gandas are stealing firewood from the nearby forest and selling it in nearby irrigated villages, or in the colony itself and earn about ten rupees a day. Shortly, ten of the households will be given *fal bhogi patta* (the rights to enjoy fruits) for two acres of cashew nuts cultivation. But they are not interested in that and instead, want to have land suitable for growing paddy and groundnut. Hence the effort of the government to raise their economic condition through such social forestry measures might not be successful. The Teli household has come to the colony very recently, purchased a plot of land and had been constructing a house on it. He is leasing in some land from the Brahmins.

In general, people were not satisfied with the compensation, especially the landholders, who thought that theirs was the best available land in that area. The maximum compensation per acre in that area fetched them a little over one acre of the best land in the new colony even though there is no comparison between these two categories of land. Moreover, during British period the Gountia had collaborated with the tenants to underclassify land to enable the tenants to pay less revenue so that the latter would not have to be ejected even during bad harvest. The tenants were also happy since they had to pay less revenue on a piece of land. The tenants invariably got lower compensation on the *naukari mafi* land. The Brahmin Gountia, and the Kulta shareholder, who had four daughters staying in different places outside the colony, could not get the compensation, due to Gountia rights, because it was not possible for them to assemble together on different occasions. The Block Chairman Shatrughna Panda, and earlier the CPI leader Prasanna Panda, had taken up the cases of the Jhankars and Chowkidars without success. The Gouds who had been cultivating, after reclaiming, about 14 acres of land of the Gountia of a nearby village, for over 20 years, and hence fought a legal case for compensation on that land failed to get anything after spending so much on litigation. Similarly, a Kulta and a Brahmin were dissatisfied because they did not get any compensation for the small ponds that they had dug up in their fields. It was also alleged that the officers ate up the fish in the ponds belonging to the village but did not allow the villagers to do so.

The cumulative earnings from summer paddy, groundnut, petty trading in rice and bidi making have revived the economic conditions of the people of the colony to a significant extent, but it is no match for the old one. People who had ruined their health and glaze due to long sufferings during the previous years, are once again smiling back to health and prosperity, although there is significant difference among the castes. The recent prosperity has enabled the people to observe the religious functions with some grandeur, as they had been doing earlier. After shifting to this colony and settling here for the last 30 years the people still visit their old village almost every summer when the level of water in the reservoir recedes down and portions of the old village is seen. Sometimes they go right up to the old location and the young ones are shown it by the older ones. The Majhians of the village, who after staying in the colony for a year or so, went back to the periphery of the reservoir, treat the people of their own village, on such occasion, with lot of fish. The occasional visit to the old village, the propitiation of the deity of the old village — with their corresponding symbols — and the unanimous tone of the old villagers that they would go back to their old village if the Hirakud Dam bursts, project the strong attachment of the people for their native place. There is not much craze for ward-membership and there has never been any election for this post. It has always been decided in informal meetings. In spite of economic differences and occasional disagreement on issues, the colony gives a well-knit picture. Except the physical layout, the cropping pattern, and occupational diversification, the inequality of the old village seems to have been reconstructed in the new colony.

(B) The Heterogeneous Resettlement Colony

Kashipali resettlement colony is 25 km. from Sambalpur, 3 km. from Rengali, 2 km. from the nearest main road and 20 km. South of the Kudopali colony. It is a part of the Nua Rampella colony complex and has been named so because most of the people of the colony have come from Kashipali. Kulta, Bhuyans, Mirdhas and Gandas of Jampali; Chamars of Rampella; Gandas of Fatapali; and others from Taldihi, Purna, Ramila, Ban Sagar and Antarduli constitute the population of the present population of Kashipali colony. All these villages were on the East Bank of river Ib, that is, just on the other side of Kudopali. Some of these villages were very close to each other, as in the case of Kashipali and Jampali, and the villagers had some idea about the people of the neighbouring villages. Land in all these villages, and especially in Kashipali and Jampali, was very fertile and the people were not having any problem regarding the basic necessities of life. People grew paddy, sugarcane, gram, horsegram, vegetables, water-melon, castor, bhang and ganja in plenty. Kashipali was famous for sugarcane. The yield rate was very high and higher than in double-cropped area of recent times. Fish were available in plenty round-the-year and in rainy season the villages smelt of fish. Since the Gountia of Kashipali-Jampali belonged to village Sankarma at some distance, the cultivators were in a position to get land in lease and share-cropping and hence able-bodied people never faced any economic hardship.

People from these villages, who went else where have not been concentrated in one colony but in numerous old established villages and stayed mostly with their relatives, especially with fathers-in-law or with maternal uncles. Brahmins from the old villages did not come here because they were very apprehensive about agricultural production in the new soil. They anticipated a lot of difficulties in the initial years when they would not have sufficient resources to employ labourers and face labour scarcity. The labourers were not likely to be available because they might be busy in constructing their houses and reclaiming their own land, if at all. They also wanted to go to towns to become priest, cook, betel-shop-owner, vendor, businessman, contractor, rentier, clerk, teacher, etc. This is because they had the necessary skill, education and resources to pursue these occupations and professions. The decision to come to this colony, after visiting several other would-be-colonies, was finally taken by a Mirdha, two Kultas, the Bhuyan Jhankar and the Ganda Chowkidar when these five people observed *binnhi* and *panasi* (wild grass), and *thelko* (a jungle fruit) in abundance in this locality and thought it to be very suitable for agricultural production. There was a *nalia* (rivulet) from which water could be lifted for growing vegetables and sugarcane. The most important factors, however, were the cheapness of the new land especially for the poor people, and its strategic location : in terms of getting year-round employment at the various upcoming industries at Rengali and even at Sambalpur and Jharsuguda, if necessary. Rengali had some important facilities like railway station, hospital, markets and businessmen, also. Further, Shatrughna Panda, an influential educated man and the-then Gountia of Rampella village, was the first to shift and stay in a newly made school building in this camp, and assured the people that there would be proper rehabilitation in this camp.

People of these villages had similar experiences, as in Kudopali, when they heard about the construction of the dam — disbelief, discussion, thinking, inactivity, demonstration and finally succumb to government's decision. These people were, however, more active than people of Kudopali because Budhuram Dube and Prasanna Panda two active leaders, against the construction of the dam, came from this locality. Dube finally backed out after some 'reward', but Panda, the CPI, MLA, is still fighting for the rehabilitation of the oustees. The manipulation and nature of complaints in the payment of compensation of land, house, trees and other structures, are similar to that of Kudopali. But the compensation for the reputed Mahadev temple of Kashipali (about Rs. 60,000) is still lying with the government. Since the Gountia did not come here, the idols are lying at Sankarma, and the temple is not being constructed here for lack of initiative and fund.

Since Kashipali colony is just about 20 km. from Kudopali colony and situated in the same geo-climatic area and there was no differential treatment in their rehabilitation, people's experiences in these two colonies should not be much different. The difference lies mostly in terms of social composition of the people, location, and availability of land and water. At Kudopali, most of the people got their compensation in the village and only a few at Sambalpur, and most of them deposited the money for land in the old village itself. At Kashipali colony most of the people got their compensation in their old villages but none of them deposited it there; some of them deposited at Sambalpur and most of them deposited in the new colony. They were allotted the land after they had settled here for two years. Hence, the caste-class alignments in terms of land is not that sharper as in Kudopali. There is a clear cut division in Kudopali regarding quality of land and its irrigability. The situation is different, if not reversible here. In the first year, people in this colony, did not cultivate the land at all because they went on constructing their houses, reclaiming their land, and kept on thinking about their old villages. They did not feel like working for agricultural production and more so because land was not allotted to them after their arrival. Next year when land was given to them on lease they cultivated, but most of them could not pay anything to the government because of poor harvest. People in old Kudopali had little land but in the colony they had sufficient land and everybody had something although the quality of land was very poor, especially for the Gandas. In old Kashipali almost all the households had some land but in the new colony many of them had to take back their money, that they had deposited with the government on the ground that sufficient land was not available in the colony. From the beginning, when allotment of land started, people started comparing with each other and complained to the Camp Officer. So people were not shown the layout of the plots allotted to them, were asked to keep silent and not to interfere with the process until the final decision was taken. However, in the mean time, some clever people befriended the officials by different mechanisms — bribe, informal gifts, loaning out cash to meet some contingency, helping and serving in domestic activities, making stay comfortable, and even arguing, after showing their support. For example, Ghasi Pradhan arranged a circulating capital of Rs. 2,000 for the Camp Officer when the latter required it urgently to pay the labourers or to meet some other contingent expenditure. He also arranged for the comfortable stay of the Camp Officer and got seven acres of contiguous patch of land, the *khari* of the colony, which unfortunately does not produce summer paddy but yields very well in the season crop. Dhanurjaya Mali got one acre of good land and a free plot by attending to the officers' kitchen, singing, gifting vegetables and by accompanying the timber trucks to Sambalpur and back, which was being sold by the Camp Officer. Two Teli households also bribed Rs. 222 and provided other helps to the officers to get 16 acre of contiguous plots 80 per cent of which is now irrigated and produces a second crop. Kangalu Ganda was very vocal and sometimes argued with Shatrughna Panda, the most influential man in this locality; had support from his caste folks and hence the Kultas asked the Camp Officers to allot him land right under the proposed tank so that wild animals would destroy his crops. Fortunately for him the tank has been constructed and later renovated and is now helping in summer paddy as a result of which his land is the most prized land in the colony.

Unlike Kudopali many people of this present colony had worked for about two years in the construction of the Hirakud dam because the distance from their villages to the worksite was maximum 10 km. Very often they were escorted back to the villages by the contractors' 'helpers' by trucks, and got higher wages because the work was risky and it had to be completed in a limited time span. As in Kudopali, people in this colony also underwent the near-starvation condition in the first ten years. In the first year people went on eating whatever they had brought from their old villages, they were mentally shattered and felt very lethargic to work; the Malis, the Telis and some of the Kultas did not work for one year; rest of them had to work compulsorily after they exhausted their stock. Some of them worked as labourers in and around the colony in the morning session and reclaimed their land or did domestic duties in the afternoon. The difficulties, in this colony, were more acute in the initial years especially because of non-availability/scarcity of water, spread of some peculiar diseases, high mortality rate, and the lack of a collective feeling to withstand the hardship, which did not come by because of the heterogeneous social composition of the colony. Caste loyalty had prevailed over the village loyalty as is evident from residential patterns in terms of caste block, even in a planned colony, but the people did not like the 'isolationist' housing pattern of the government nor did they face each other's house because of suspicion, mutual hatred and preconceived notion about the notoriety of some villagers. As compared with the people of Kudopali colony, people here have not done the work of DDT spraying, trading in cattle and selling of parched rice in Sambalpur. The new occupations pursued by them were : working in rice mills as labourers and *hemali* (load carriers); in caustic soda factory, stone crushing mill; prolonged work in road construction including stone chipping; cutting and transporting of bamboos and timber; railway coolies; and selling of leaves, tooth brush and leaf-pots by commuting in local train to Sambalpur (especially by the Gandas), and shoe-shining in local trains (by the Chamars). Given the preponderance of lower castes and tribals in this colony many of them, who had bought intangible items like gold and bicycles, had to pawn them with the Marwaris at Rengali and later forfeited those since they were not in a position to revive their economy.

Since there was acute scarcity of water in the first year trucks of water, from the reservoir, were being supplied daily for men and animals. However, the caste/tribe norm of purity and pollution was so pervasive that the upper castes like Kultas and Malis and the tribal Mirdhas did not drink or cook with this water. Many people used the yellow coloured *dhotis* which do not get polluted and hence those could be used for days together without washing. A lot of cattle died of scarcity of water and due to drinking of dirty water in distant streams. In the old villages they had a lot of buffaloes but they sold them before coming to this colony when they anticipated water scarcity. They had also to sell their goats and sheep because of the fear of wolves and hyena. During this period people were affected by an unknown fever and many people died also. The government arranged to send, in vehicles, doctors from Sambalpur and then the mortality rate came down.

Since there were not irrigated villages earlier in the neighbouring locality, labourers of this colony could not be engaged. They had to take to occupations they had never done and found it extremely difficult in the initial years. In the mills people had to work in three shifts and had to be used to heat, dust and smoke. The job was risky and more so for the people who worked as loaders and unloaders in the rice mills with steaming sackful of paddy on their backs. This was so also for the construction workers of road and stone-chippers. Many of them had to be out of action for days together for medium injuries but there was no compensation from the mill owners as all of them were on daily wage basis or on short-term contract basis and could not claim bonus, gratuity and other facilities usually available to workers in the organised sector. The routine and monotonous factory work led to disorganisation in their day-to-day life — food, sleep and agricultural activities including animal husbandry. Ladies who went to Rengali, alongwith their kids, to make bidi, which they learnt from two ladies sent to the colony by Meghna Bidi Company at Sambalpur, had to work in the presence of their kids since there were no creches. Obviously very few children could go to the L.P. School at Mangalpur. All these upset the tranquil agricultural life of the people of this colony so much so that they could not take to any activity which would have given them collective feeling. It was like 'every one for himself and away from the gallows'. During this difficult phase they could not perform the religious festivals and functions that they were organising with grandeur, in their old villages and even could not think of re-establishing the Mahadev Temple for which compensation is still lying with the government. It is interesting to observe that most of the young people of this colony look under-built and it might be worth examining whether it could have been due to malnutrition and semi-starved condition. It was reported that many of the old people died early because of over-work and mental agony. Incidentally there was just one Kulta and one Ganda beyond the age of sixty five.

Table 4.2 shows the ownership of resources in this heterogeneous colony. However, it does not show the distribution of about 25 acre of irrigated land reclaimed by 30 households; and 14 acre of dry land reclaimed by the Chamars alone. These land have been illegally encroached upon by people in the full knowledge of the Revenue officials. They have been cultivating the land for last five years or so. They have applied to the Tahasildar for permanent *patta* and they are most likely to get it after paying fine, reduced rent of a few years, and further bribe. After the availability of irrigation facilities from the tank and pond (constructed way back in 1953 and 1955 respectively) since 1971, and increasing income for the irrigated land holders there is rivalry/jealousy among the 'haves' and the 'havenots' of such land. People, whose plots are situated below and close to the tank and pond, take to the cultivation of long maturing and high yielding summer paddy for more profit thereby depriving others, who have land far off these water resources, of utilising the water even for harvesting the season crop. If short variety of paddy is grown during season

TABLE 4.2: Distribution of Resources in the Heterogeneous Resettlement Colony

Castes/ Tribes	No. of h.h.	% to the total	Total popln.	% to the total	Amt. of land (in acres) 1926	Amt. of total land (in acres) 1987	Amt. of land irrigated (in acres) 1987	% of irrigated to total land	Amt. of land per h.h. (in acres)	Bullocks in pairs	Amt. of land per pair of bullocks (in acres)
Kulta	9	8.82	41	10.02	N	24.29	16.99	69.95	2.70	8	3.04
Goud	4	3.92	21	5.13	O	12.43	8.99	72.33	3.11	3	4.14
Mali/Chhanapati	4	3.92	24	5.87	T	27.55	8.23	29.88	6.89	5	5.51
Teli	8	7.84	27	6.60	A	25.19	15.01	59.59	3.15	5	5.04
Keut	2	1.96	13	3.18	V	4.38	3.14	71.69	2.19	4	1.10
Dhuba	1	0.98	2	0.89	A	3.04	2.70	88.82	3.04	1	3.04
Luhura	2	1.96	5	1.22	I	0.83	0.55	66.27	0.42	0	—
Pap	8	7.84	34	8.31	L	13.60	8.54	62.79	1.70	2	6.80
Ganda	33	32.35	107	26.16	A	48.46	20.10	41.48	1.47	13	3.73
Chamar	8	7.84	32	7.82	B	0	0	0	0	4	—
Mirdha	8	7.84	38	9.29	L	23.17	8.29	35.78	2.90	3	7.72
Bhuyan	12	11.76	50	12.22	E	22.03	8.45	38.36	1.84	11	2.00
Gond	3	2.94	15	3.67		13.67	8.27	60.50	4.56	2	6.84
Total	102	99.97	409	100.38	—	218.64	109.26	49.97	2.14	61	3.58

crop, more amount of summer paddy can be cultivated, utilising the excess water of the tanks. Further, if less acreage of summer paddy is cultivated, the water can be utilised for growing more of groundnut, gram, sugarcane, wheat, potato, tomato, bean and ladies-finger, as some people have been doing with considerable profit. This would benefit more people also. Like Kudopali, in this colony also, one side of the land is not irrigated at all but half of it can grow such crops if water can be allowed to flow through a cement tube or wooden tube constructed at a cost of a few thousand rupees. For four years people utilised water for growing vegetables, etc. when government had provided the necessary temporary arrangements. However, once that needed some repairing, people did not take interest in repairing it. Some people who wanted to grow more summer paddy took away in the night the asbestos sheets and wooden planks, etc. used in that over-bridge canal. The nearness to semi-urban centres means more profit from vegetables but the greed of some people has deprived others of every thing.

The occupational pattern of the caste groups has undergone significant changes, some of which we have already noted. Even during the worst days the clean castes have not taken to polluting activities, but in the factories and mills they have worked side-by-side and sometimes shoulder-to-shoulder with the polluting castes. Besides agriculture the Kultas have taken to shop-keeping, blue-collar work, petty contractory, carpentry and rearing and selling of bullocks and goats. Their economising behaviour and hard labour have enabled them to gradually come up in the economic ladder. The Malis have not been earning anything from their traditional occupation, i.e., worshipping at Mahadev temple and *dakshina* from the devotees. They took to labour activities that they had never done. They earn something from the sale of milk and renting out their carts and also working in blue-collar works. The Telis are no more pressing oil seeds as there is an oil-mill at Rengali and also because there are not many mahua trees around, neither there is much cultivation of til and mustard. More over, people have shown preference for mill-made refined oil. So the well off ones are taking to agriculture; the poor ones have taken to labour and petty trading in vegetables, fish and other items needing small investment. One of them is also a Village Health Guide (VHG) and makes some money by selling the medicines, supposed to be freely distributed, and injecting people. In this SCs/STs dominated colony who constitute 75 per cent population and who do not necessarily need the services of the washerman, the Dhoba's earning is virtually zero from the traditional work. Fortunately they have some land and they are managing smoothly on agriculture and little jajmani work. The Keuts have not been able to sell as much parched rice as they are expected to because the upper castes and tribals are doing so at home. Again they are not earning anything from fishing which was their most important occupation in the old village. Difficulties of collecting firewood from the nearby forest has also discouraged them from making parched rice for the urban consumers. The Luhura household has virtually left the blacksmithery work and is depending on liquor retailing and theft of metallic items for making and selling of finished goods. No Ganda is weaving clothes in this colony whereas 30 per cent of them used to weave coarse clothes in the old villages. They are still taking to sale of firewood, tooth-brush and leaves which they collect from the nearby forest. Besides agriculture they take to all sorts of labour activities. The Chamars, who stay in a separate block and at a distance from the colony, have cleared about 14 acres of land that produces the season crop. They did not have any land in the old village. These are the people who have comparatively prospered most in the new setting because they were free to take any sort of activity which is looked down upon by others. They suffered from one handicap : while they sell their rice dehulled by themselves they cannot sell it in the local market but they do it in distant markets. They could have prospered further but for their drinking habits. Besides agriculture and other activities, they are still doing their traditional occupations like scavenging and related activities (leather works). They also do shoe-shinning and repairing in weekly markets and in the shuttle train between Sambalpur and Jharsuguda. Among the tribals the family of the Bhuyan Jhankar and his kinsmen are little well off; rest of them are so so. Some of them are living from hand-to-mouth. Many of them have been cheated while getting the compensation and they could not utilise the money properly. The shock of uprooting immobilised them in the initial years. They were late starters in new economic opportunities; they have also less irrigated land compared to other social groups in the colony. Drinking habit in general, has affected the tribals and the Scheduled Castes. It is significant to observe the long luggage-carriers of the bicycles in these colonies, including Kudopali, which shows that they do petty trading in different items. There is no white-collar worker in this colony and nobody has passed Matriculation even though they have the High School and the College only at a distance of 3 km. It shows that children could not be spared for such long-term 'luxury'.

Since people of different villages have flocked in here, it would be interesting to enquire as to what has happened to the social fabric of this colony 30 years after its formation. Starting from the allotment of land there was feeling in terms of inter-village, inter-caste, inter-tribe difference — which later manifested in the construction of the main doors of the house not facing the rivals and later culminating in intra-caste/tribe division depending on economic resources. Meetings have been generally poorly organised. Nobody's word has been given sufficient weight and there has hardly been any consensus on any important issue. Even in simple clear-cut case justice is denied to the sufferer, usually the poor, because the rich ones mobilise support in their favour. Influential people, especially from the major villages Kashipali and Jampali, have been encroaching on government land and when people from other villages, and especially the poor ones, started doing so they dissuaded them on the pretext that the plots have already been earmarked for reclamation. Similarly, the influential ones who have managed to get land below the water resources rarely look into the interest of the people who have land at the tail end and usually do not allow the latter to take water from the tanks, through a separate channel in their land. This has been the bone of contention on many occasions. Within the colony there have been many cases of theft, deliberate destruction of crops by men and cattle, swindling of collective funds, illegitimate pregnancies, abduction and elopements, rape, desertions, attempt to murder, alleged hypnotism, wide-spread practice of witchcraft, etc. which are generally considered as deviant behaviour in villages of this district. There have been many cases of police coming to this colony implying that the people have not been in a position to sort out the matters amicably amongst themselves in meetings. The colony does not portray any community feeling except probably during the organisation of *Nam Yajna* but after the occasion there is always accusation/allegation regarding misuse/misappropriation of fund. In recent times the Gandas have been discriminated when they touched the prasad in a religious festival and since then they have been organising their own *Nam Yajna* even though it means a collection of Rs. 50 plus per household, which is roughly equivalent to the wage of a man for a week. The people of this colony, as in all the colonies, have been too much dependent on government for the maintenance of facilities/construction provided by the government as in the case of renovation of well, pond and the over-bridge canal. As in Nua-Mura Camp, here also people of different colonies with in a complex, have been sharing common forest and grazing land. This has led to inter-colony rivalry and people of this colony are termed notorious. On the other hand, the inhabitants of this colony allege that since the Block Chairman, who has been in that post through out, is staying at Rampella colony, most of the facilities are being available there and in excessive proportion (which seems to be true in terms of concentration of population).

Nearness to Rengali town has helped to bring out a few matric-plucked students in this colony, who are now looking for a way out to quench their frustration of unemployment in white/blue-collar works which they had desired for. In 1985 they collected Rs. 2 per month for six months, from a few households to form a registered *Yubak Sangha* and then take to developmental works, contract works, etc. This was not liked by the old ones who sensed deviant behaviour in them. The Bhuyan head-man, a petty-contractor, also nullified their efforts since that would have hampered his interest.

Despite better land, more amount of irrigated land distributed over all social groups, and much better location in terms of opportunities vis-a-vis Kudopali colony, it does not portray of a cohesive unit. The people explain it in terms of the absence of 'cultured' Brahmins and the *panch rasi* character of the colony, i.e., of a heterogeneous population.

Comparison

A comparison of the two colonies leads us to believe that people of both the colonies underwent a lot of difficulties for the first 15 years of their resettlement in the new localities, which differed significantly from their native villages in terms of physical layout, topography, cropping pattern; availability of water, fish, grazing land; and social composition of the neighbouring villages. In both the colonies there have been dissatisfaction in the allotment of land. In the homogeneous colony the amount of land available was more than that of the heterogeneous colony but in both the colonies there was/is animosity between the Kultas and the Gandas and in both the colonies the Gandas have been discriminated by the higher castes primarily because of the aggressive nature of the Gandas. People of both the colonies could withstand the difficulties of the initial years because of the availability of forest resources, agricultural labour in villages within reasonable distance, bidi works; and later petty-trading in rice, and cultivation of a second crop of paddy, sugarcane, groundnut, vegetables and pulses, etc. The nearness to railway station, business centres and industries allowed the people of the heterogeneous colony to have income from non-agricultural sources also. Even though the distribution of irrigated land (presently) is more dispersed over castes in the heterogeneous colony and there is considerable occupational diversification, the colony lacks 'life' because of the heterogeneous nature of the people and divided interest and loyalties. There is division both within the castes, tribes and within the people of a particular erstwhile village, and there is no clear pattern of group formation even though faction has been the very basis of underdevelopment in this locality.

Even though government used the same principles for the rehabilitation of the people of these two colonies, the people adopted different means for starting life afresh. Consequently the present social formation of the two colonies has been different primarily because of the different social composition and also because of the availability of different opportunities in these two localities.

NOTES

1. According to Act No.18 of Land Acquisition Act, 1948, and the Orissa Development of Industries, Irrigation, Agriculture, Capital Construction and Resettlements of Displaced Persons (Land Acquisition) Rules, 1950, compensation was given to the owner of the land in the following manner : The compensation for *rayati* land, during 1948-53, was 500 times the deduced rent of the plot. For *bhogra* land, the same formula was applicable. In 1960, *bhogra* land was paid 16 year's net produce where net produce is equivalent to total output minus 50 per cent of the expenditure (production cost). It was estimated that gross production in *bahal*, *benna*, *mal*, and *aat* type of land was respectively 22, 22, 15 and 7 maunds of paddy. For every 22 maunds of paddy, 33 maunds of straw was estimated. The rate of paddy was Rs. 9 per maund and that of straw Rs. 2 per maund. From 1948 to 1953, the compensation for each acre of *bahal*, *benna*, *mal* and *aat* variety was Rs. 500, 300, 120 and 50 respectively. This procedure was not followed strictly and for *aat* land people received compensation as low as Rs. 18.75 per acre at a time when the government paid Rs. 10 per day per pair of bullocks hired from Punjab for clay compressing purpose (Supakar, 1988 : 21-22).

2. People were pressurised not to go for arbitration case. If they went the applications were every often, suppressed. With reference to the Orissa Assembly, starred question no. 3738 dated 13/12/1955 the Chief Minister himself had replied that 287 cases had not been referred to the Arbitration and most of them were pending for more than one year.
3. After complaints, each truck was provided with a security guard and the evacuees had to sign that they reached their destinations safely; otherwise the drivers did not get their remuneration.
4. Evacuation, by the HLO, started on 14th April '55 and by 4th June '55, 33 full villages and 13 part villages with 4000 families had been evacuated. There were transit camps at Rampella, Baghmunda, Kantapali, Kutripali, Rampaluga and Adhapada, etc. There were strong resistance from people of Sagarpali and Adhapada. See (Government of Orissa : Political and Services (RVD), 1957 : 10). From the answer of the starred qn. no. 2165 dated 14/8/1955 at Orissa Assembly it is clear that three platoons of armed Police force were marched to frighten people against resistance.
5. During such time people used ferry boats to take out their children and women folk, to go to the other side of the river for passing stool, and for collecting logs from the river.
6. For the cattle market at Sakti, in Madhya Pradesh, they covered the distance mostly by train while going, but walked back the entire distance along with the bullocks and buffaloes. They started on Tuesday and reached Sambalpur on Sunday to sell the cattle, and came back home on Sunday evening only. The transaction time was usually between November to May when the rivers had little water in them and paddy crop was no more in the field.
7. However, they recalled the murder of a lame Brahmin bachelor, who was a prosperous shopkeeper. He was done to death by a tribal hired by a Kulta. The incident, however, did not lead to any strained relationship between the Brahmins and the Kultas.
8. L.S.S.O' Malley (1909) also mentions about the infamous Gandas of the Bargarh area who used to rob the passengers on the way.
9. When the other households of Brahmin, Kulta and Ganda caste from other sub-merged villages, and a Teli household from Cuttack district, came to settle in this colony they could not be adjusted in such caste-blocks.
10. For a simple cost-benefit analysis of the domestic rice-husking and the impact of mechanisation on this industry see, Baboo (1988 : 251-64).

5

PERIPHERAL REHABILITATION OF TWO OFF-SHORE VILLAGES : Partly Submerged Vs. Fully Submerged

In the previous Chapter we have noted that people in the colonies were not very happy with the rehabilitational scheme of the government. Most importantly the oustees did not like to settle in forest-cleared land because they were very close to rivers and plain land with higher productivity, and led rather an easy life as far as earning livelihood was concerned. They found the life in the resettlement colonies so difficult that they have, very often, left the colonies for other localities and sometimes abandoned the colony completely, as in the case of Udsung resettlement colony. On the other hand, the government was also not in a position to provide substantial amount of forest-cleared land, temporary houses and other essential facilities in suitable area for the oustees; nor was it in a position to rehabilitate them in old established villages where land was a scarce commodity. When the efforts of the government failed in such arrangement and the date for filling-up the reservoir came close by, the government was compelled to persuade/allow the inhabitants between RL 630-632 to stay back in their old villages as far as possible, or to shift a little so that the village was not at all submerged but the land might or might not get submerged. Partial rehabilitation of this nature is called peripheral or off-shore resettlement.

In this section we would be concerned with rehabilitation of people of two villages who have experienced such partial rehabilitation. Pudhapara and Sapne are two villages situated on the East bank of river Ib at a distance of 12 km. from each other. Due to construction of the Hirakud dam and flooding of the reservoir the whole of the village and most of the land of Sapne got submerged and people shifted a little from the original location. At Pudhapara the village *abadi* (homestead land) remained intact but 70 per cent of the total land got submerged, it came under RL 632. It might be interesting to compare the reconstruction of life in these two villages after we discuss them individually.

(A) The Partly Submerged Off-shore Village

Pudhapara is 1 km. away from the Sambalpur-Jharsuguda main road and connected by a motorable fair weather road 5 km. from Rengali and 2 km. from Lapanga, the two railway stations. Most of the government and semi-government offices which relate to the finance and administration of the village, are situated at Rengali and Lapanga. The weekly markets are also held there. Before the submergence of most of the land of the village, due to the construction of the dam, the village was famous for the production of high quality paddy, sugarcane, gram, mango and custard apple, and for the Samalai deity and Chandan Yatra. The location of the village in the middle of the trade route between Sambalpur and Jharsuguda had given it a special significance which was eroded by its sub-mergence, and the construction of the highway. There were quite a few prosperous tenants in this village and 30 annually attached labourers (*gutis*) mostly belonging to the Ganda, the Gond, the Keut and the Goud communities. The Brahmins, Kultas and Sundhis employed these *gutis*. The village had tanks, ponds and rivers on three sides and the land was highly fertile and plain. The crop production hardly failed in normal years. There was more than sufficient fruit and fodder available for men and cattle. However, the plight of the agricultural labourers was pitiable because they solely depended on their employers in the village and did not have any opportunities for non-agricultural occupation around.

When notice about the submergence of the land and compensation came, and it became clear that the prosperous sections of the people were to lose most of their land, the poorer sections were very anxious because they anticipated unemployment in the event of the prosperous ones leaving the village. The Brahmin Gountia had land in other villages also, but he wanted to retain land, as far as possible, in this village because of the good name of the village and because it was a *Brahmottar mafi* (rent-free village held in lieu of priestly services) village where he had several rights, which had been taken away in other villages, after the abolition of the Zamindari system. So he persuaded the villagers to stay back on the full assurance that the waters of the reservoir would not swell to the level announced by the government, that the Samalai temple, the pride of the village was not going to be sub-merged, and the residential site would remain intact.

The Gountia was respected by the villagers, and they trusted him. On the other hand, the government also persuaded the villagers to stay back on the assurance that the remaining land and the land that fell between RL 630-632 would be distributed among them, and that they would be absorbed in many new employment schemes. The poor, who did not have land, or had very little land, were convinced by this persuasion. But, for the households who had substantial holdings and who ultimately lost about 80 per cent of their land, it was a crucial decision. The land that remained was inferior upland, grazing land, village shrubs and forest which would yield hardly anything. These people were used to a particular standard of life and could not think in terms of expansion of their land by leasing in or purchase; they believed that they would not be in a position to better themselves by any means, if they stayed in the village, and so took the decision to leave the village. But their decision came too late. By then the value of land had already appreciated to some extent in the unaffected areas and they got the last of the pick when they went to the Basiapara Camp, because some of their relatives from other villages went there. Of these households eight came back to the village and two stayed in the village but not on their own land: they went on looking around for land, bought new land and constructed houses or stayed in relatives' houses and cultivated land. They moved out late because after getting compensation for their land which had been acquired by the government, they could not get compensation for their houses, until they demolished those houses, and went about disposing the remaining land in the village or leasing it out. Those who stayed back took advantage of this situation since they knew that the 'oustees' who had already taken the compensation and planned to settle else where could neither come back to collect the dues for leased out land nor do anything even if they were not paid the dues. The more enterprising among them forcibly cultivated their land or on the false promise that they would pay a fixed amount for the lease, but they did not purchase the land as such. The villagers who had decided to leave the village suffered substantial other losses as well besides those noted earlier. While making arrangement for new land and accommodation, they spent a large part of their compensation money. In some cases, even after purchasing land these people were not in a position to take possession of the land, i.e., they could not get the *patta* (record of rights), because of the SC/ST status and the minor (*nabalak*) status of the owner of the land who complained later on to the Tahsildar. In one case a Brahmin was pick-pocketed of Rs. 7000 in the bus while going to purchase a piece of land, and had to resell the piece of land after a few years when his old parents back at home needed urgent medical attention. In another case a man came back from the registration court when he heard that high voltage electric lines would go over the piece of land, which he had decided to buy. Since he had already paid 60 per cent of the total money in advance which had been already spent by the prospective seller he suffered a loss. Encroachment on the housing and garden sites of 'oustees' was widespread so that the 'oustees' were often not able to restructure their houses on the original sites even if they came back to the village; in some cases they could regain their houses and land after donating some money to the village fund. Once they left the village they were considered outsiders and were not welcomed back to the village since others had some vested interests in the property they had left behind. This was because after the submergence land had become an even more scarce item.

The people had been told that the water of the dam would come up to RL 630 every year and sometimes up to RL 632. They were instructed not to cultivate land below RL 630, but they could cultivate land between RL 630 and RL 632 at their own risk. Initially, people cultivated as much as they could only to find that they were not in a position to harvest the season crop in November-December, for the reservoir was almost full and there was neck-deep water in the fields. Three years after sub-mergence, i.e., in 1960 the government allowed the people to cultivate on a lease basis. The Revenue Inspector made it clear to the villagers that there was no principle regarding the allotment of such land leases (between RL 630-632) and fore-shore leases (below RL 630). The amount of land leased out and its location depended on bribe, influence and the prior social standing of the concerned person (see Table 5.1). In this also some people were deprived because they were out of station during the allotment days, or as in one case attending to dying persons, or they could not afford the amount for lease. In 1984, the Gountia had to surrender 15 acres of his ceiling surplus land, which was of course, the most unproductive portion, and it was distributed among 'deserving people' in the village. Here also the rules were violated. The oustees from the village, who came back, were given the last priority in such allotment on the assumption that they had had land for which they had already been given compensation. None from the village, except the Gountia, who himself was a lawyer, got compensation on arbitration. People took whatever they were offered because they were wary of the expenses on litigation, the delay, uncertainties, etc. They were so naive that when the officers came for crop-cutting to ascertain the compensation, they showed the most inferior portions in that type of land; they thought that agricultural tax could be imposed if the most productive portion was shown.

As it has been noted earlier the people were not told the motive behind a particular action of the officials. This village had one advantage vis-a-vis the villages discussed in the last Chapter, that even after announcement of the dam construction and sub-mergence people did not get that panicked because their village was not going to be sub-merged and that they would not be shelterless at least. It would not be proper, however, to say that they were happy. As regards the lease it was not permanent or transferable : if a man failed to pay the dues, left the village or died it was reallotted. Moreover, since it is sub-mergible land people did not/would not take to investment in such land and hence the productivity was less than what it should be. The silt deposited by the flood in the reservoir helps the productivity, in some years, but the uncertainty in the land lease is too high. If the people cultivate tall and long maturing paddy and if the water level does not touch RL 632 in a particular year, then it suffers from lack of water (*pudi*) and hence results in low/no yield. On the other hand, if short and short-maturing paddy is cultivated and the flood level touches RL – 632, then the crop gets sub-merged (*budi*) and destroyed. They have not been able to grow any variety of paddy which is not affected by such factors.[1]

The flooding of the land, especially the banks of the rivers of the old village, has deprived people of very valuable trees, fruit and fodder. The sub-mergence also led to the displacement of the influential and rich people of the surrounding villages thereby leaving them without leaders and resources. It led to the suspension of much of the collective work they had been doing earlier, for a number of years, until the emergence of a new leadership and a new resource base. The resources were available after the villagers got employment in non-agricultural activities along with cultivating the available land.

TABLE 5.1: Distribution of Resources in the Partly Sub-merged Village

Castes/ Tribes	No. of h.h	% to the total	Total Popln.	% to the total	Total land in 1925 (in acres)	Total Rayati land (in acres) 1980	Fore-shore lease (in acres) 1986	Land lease (in acres) 1986	Total land (in acres) 1986	Amt. of land per h.h (in acres)	Bullocks (in pairs)	Amt. of land per pair of bullocks (in acres)
Brahmin	2	2.35	11	2.68	176.66	33.56	3.80	0.64	38.00	19.00	2	19.00
Kulta	5	5.88	38	9.27	112.87	12.26	5.30	4.37	29.93	5.99	8	3.74
Goud	7	8.24	40	9.76	6.25	2.20	2.50	4.58	9.28	1.33	7	1.33
Teli	5	5.88	28	6.83	16.40	0.08	0.60	0.56	1.24	0.25	2	0.62
Sundhi	4	4.71	15	3.66	63.55	1.74	0	0.93	2.67	0.67	3	0.89
Sial	2	2.35	18	4.39	0	0.19	0.50	0.62	1.31	0.66	2	0.66
Keut	14	16.47	58	14.15	46.82	8.33	6.35	4.62	19.30	1.38	5	3.86
Dhuba	7	8.24	35	8.54	0	0.05	2.35	3.08	5.48	0.78	2	2.74
Bhandari	1	1.18	7	1.71	0.77	0	1.15	1.22	2.37	2.37	0	—
Ganda	18	21.18	65	15.85	29.46	3.35	11.10	7.64	22.09	1.23	10	2.21
Dom	1	1.18	3	0.73	0	0.12	0.50	0	0.62	0.62	0	—
Chamar	0	0	0	0	21.68	2.83	0	0	2.83	—	0	—
Sahara	5	5.88	28	6.83	7.11	0.12	1.50	4.16	5.78	1.16	3	1.93
Gond	14	16.47	64	15.61	32.87	1.64	1.65	8.05	11.34	0.81	6	1.89
Total	85	100.01	410	100.01	517.44	66.47	37.30	40.47	152.24	1.79	50	3.04

Their fragmented activities, freedom from some sort of subjugation — especially for the attached labourers — and the absence of a father-figure do not portray a stable picture. It is today a faction-ridden village. After the sub-mergence the Gountia entrusted three attached labourers of the village, one of them an intelligent and experienced one, to look after his land and house, and went to stay at Sambalpur. He comes to the village usually during *Samalai Puja* and sometimes during harvest. The villagers still depend on him for important decisions.

After the allotment of the lease land in 1960, there were continuous floods for three years and during this period the people suffered heavy losses in agriculture. Almost all of them had to mortgage and later forfeit items like gold, utensils, etc. to the Marwaris and Kansaris (bell-metal makers) at Rengali. During this period, only the Brahmin Gountia and another Brahmin household were in a position to have attached labourers. The occupational pattern of the people of this village underwent a radical change after this crisis. The Brahmin Gountia who had received a substantial amount of compensation, and whose children are highly educated have taken to professional activities after initial stay at Sambalpur. The other Brahmin household leased out their limited land (and even today occasionally cultivate a portion of their land) and took up jobs in the Revenue Deptt., the Livestock Deptt. and even coal mines because they were a little educated. Alongwith their income from land they manage somehow with their salary and the substantial amount of gold and silver they had prior to sub-mergence. The remaining villagers took up various jobs which they were capable of and which they thought would be most paying : kendu leave plucking (1955 onwards) during spring for 40 days, bidi making (1970 onwards), fishing and fish-trading for about 8 to 10 months in a year, in the reservoir after 1960, road construction, work in rice mills, soda and lime factories, stone crushers; selling of *benacher* (a root used in chics), etc. Surprisingly, they did not take to selling of parched-rice outside the village or petty trading in rice, even though the rice mill is just 5 km. away. Only two Keuts have taken to selling of parched-rice at Sambalpur and two others had been petty trading in vegetables. Proximity to the town has also helped in education but nobody had studied beyond matriculation. Two Brahmins and three Dhubas worked in rice-hullers, three Telis in the railway deptt., two Gouds in a re-factory, one Kulta in a colliery, one as a police constable and two boys as domestic servants of the relative of the Gountia at Rourkela, and a Sundhi as the *munshi* (assistant) in a kendu leaves concern. Only two Ganda households, out of ten, who were weaving coarse cloth earlier continue to do so. They manage the operations on their own and not through any Weavers' Cooperatives. A Ganda and a Gond are engaged in supplying fish to traders at Sambalpur and Jharsuguda, who in turn, send these to Rourkela and Tatanagar. Eight persons work as attached labourers in the nearby villages.

Before sub-mergence the concentration of wealth was amongst the Brahmins, the Kultas and the Sundhis. The ownership of land has more or less been equalised after the provision of lease and 'implementation' of ceiling. Hence people with extra income from salaried jobs, business and intensive cultivation are becoming richer. A Goud, a Kulta and a Teli, who have lift pumps, and a Dhuba household — with salaried personnel — have become richer compared to the rest of the villagers. Again people who have been in a position to cultivate summer paddy below the pond since 1970, and encroached on land on the bank of the nearby river (with the help of irrigation pumps) are earning good income. The labourers, who led a miserable life earlier, are noticeably better off; They have become free and are in a position to earn Rs. 8 to Rs. 10 per day per head if they are physically fit and are motivated to work. Able-bodied people no longer starve. However, in recent times the mechanisation process in the rice mills has displaced a large number of labourers — an operation which required 20 persons, is being managed by just two — and is affecting the employment opportunities of the villagers. So increasingly they are depending on bidi making which pays them Rs. 8.50 per 1000 bidis and they can earn up to Rs. 12 per head per day. Since the people have manageable land for agricultural operation and there is no transplantation of the season crop there is some mutual exchange of labour and livestock for various operations and none, except the Gountia, employ hired labour. But since other works come to an almost grinding halt during the rainy season, the labourers and poor peasants travel to distant irrigated villages, close to the main road, for various agricultural operations, such as transplanting and weeding. They usually travel by truck, paying some fare or free-of-charge or on foot. Sometimes they camp in those villages for a few days if their families at home manage on their own.

Since, by this time, the poor peasants would have almost exhausted their paddy, after investment in agriculture, and the labourers really need wages in kind — which comes through agricultural labour — all of them prefer it even though it means getting a lower wage, travelling a long distance, returning late in the evenings on muddy, slushy roads, and getting drenched in the rain. Seeking jobs outside the village — by both men and women — has led to neglect of children and their education, disorganisation in family life, and lack of collective free time except late in the night for meeting, social gatherings, etc. Neglect of children's education means significant dropouts and those children are learning to tend the cattle, collect cowdung and make bidis. Given the problem of unemployment in the town area itself, it is unlikely that the non-matriculates of this village will ever get semi-skilled jobs in towns, in the future, as they have somehow managed to get now. In the face of limited land, labour displacement mechanisms, and increasing population, the villagers might have a tough time if the government prohibits them from cultivating the lease land. The government has already told them not to cultivate the fore-shore lease land because cultivation loosens the soil, silts the reservoir and leads to a lot of loss. When asked, people said that they would continue to cultivate the leased land until the government imprisoned them as that had become an important source of their livelihood.

Scarcity of firewood has become an important problem in the village but people have been bribing the forest guards to collect firewood for personal use. They also collect firewood during the first flood in the nearby river and when the reservoir is filled up because dried logs float ashore. Shortage of firewood has led people to cut down fruit-bearing trees on the ceiling surplus land. It is rather surprising to note that despite the tall claims of the government on rural upliftment, the villagers hardly succeed in getting loans from the PACS, the LDB and other Banks for agriculture, fishing and petty trading. Only 10 people have so far been financed by the PACS for crop loan and all of them are defaulters. Since most of the people have lease land with no *patta*, there is nothing to be attached to obtain a short-term loan from the PACS. The loans financed for cloth-shops, goattery, cycles and tailoring machines, etc. have been utter failures. The people have a lot of complaints against the officials viz. bribery, having to run around, poor stock and harassment. It is however, more surprising that there are lot of applicants who are dissatisfied because they had not been financed for a boat and a net, which would require about Rs. 4,000 per head, because there is less risk in this occupation and the location of the village affords a lot of scope for fishing. Recently taxation on fishing has become a disincentive too.

The village is being increasingly faction-ridden by a few touts : the main issue is the cultivation of summer paddy without any contribution to the village fund and without any rent being paid to the government, the discrimination against the Gandas which began with the *Samalai Puja* (the worship of the main deity of the village) and the high-handed attitude of the Telis.[2] Although, there are a few vocal members who are also well-off, the people do not abide by their decision. The Gandas do not attend the village meetings these days because they were given insufficient attention on earlier occasions. Moreover, their offerings of a goat to the deity Samalai were not accepted by the other villagers. So they organise religious functions like *Nam Yajna* separately. It is important to note that in Kudopali, Kashipali and also in Pudhapara, the Gandas have been discriminated against and that they have been very vocal, at least in the last two localities. The clean castes (non-SC/ST) have been speaking vehemently against the facilities provided to the SC/ST and they are increasingly opposed to and envious of them. This might ultimately lead to some sort of a caste rather than a class war.

Another aspect that needs attention in these three localities is that for a few years the people had felt acutely deprived, when because of their sacrifices, people in Pahil Par (on the other side of the river Mahanadi) had double-cropped cultivation, and they being on the bank of the river suffered a lot. It was mitigated to some extent when some of them could cultivate summer paddy. Further more, the villagers are unhappy as in all these villages the government has taken to plantation of cashew-nut and *subabul* (a kind of fodder) and distributing it to the SCs/STs, thereby depriving people of grazing land, and even a place to defecate.

(B) The Fully Sub-merged Off-shore Village

Sapne, a village comprising nearly 50 households in 1955, with a total area of 919.82 acres in 1925, and situated on the East bank of river Ib is 27 km. away from Sambalpur, 35 km. from Jharsuguda and 7 km. from Rengali. It is connected with the main road by 7 km. long all weather non-metalled road but does not have any direct bus connection, which is a distinct disadvantage compared to the three localities discussed so far. Rampella was the biggest village just across the river. The village was very close to Mahula-Bhanja forest and hence the people did not have any problem obtaining forest produce, firewood and fodder. The village produced plenty of rice, gram, white pea, *bhang* (the powder used in making bidi), castor, til and some sugarcane and vegetables. Despite congenial facilities people did not grow substantial vegetables because of wild animals. The village also had mango, mahua, date and palm trees. Fish was available in plenty round-the-year and people brew their own liquors from mahua and rice. It was a multi-caste village and the Brahmin Gountia was an absentee staying at Jogipali at a distance of one km. The people depended primarily on agriculture, weaving, bell-metal works, fishing, selling of forest produce, milk and milk products. Most of the Gonds and Gandas worked as attached and casual labourers of the Brahmins, the Bhulias and the Kansaris. It was reported that the prosperity poverty distinction was so clear in Sapne that if the dam had not been constructed, by 1965, almost all the present villagers would have been working as attached labourers under the Brahmins after mortgaging the limited land that they had. Since people of the lower castes and tribals used liquor almost regularly the Brahmins used common tricks like usury, litigation and instigation of people to spend more on non-productive activities, and gradually alienated the poor of their land. About 45 households had straw-thatched houses reflecting their poverty. Even though the village was situated on the bank of the river, the water was used only during October-January; it was not usable in rainy season because of the high content of mud, and in summer because the scanty water in the river was highly polluted by the industrial refuse of the Orient Paper Mills (OPM) situated at Brajrajnagar.

During 1948-52, four Khadias and two Gandas of this village worked in the Hirakud dam but later stopped because many people died during the construction. It was alleged that people were being sacrificed in the night or forced to perform work involving high risk thereby resulting in death. One leper colony was alleged to have been sacrificed completely. Most of the people had participated in the anti-Hirakud dam demonstration held at Sambalpur and more so because many of them went to Rampella everyday, which was one of the important centres of the anti-Hirakud dam movement, and heard the news/rumours about the dam. However, the villagers did not resist when the government asked them to vacate. By the time the eviction notice was served, most of the people had little land, having been deprived of the land by the Brahmins; hence they received little compensation. The Brahmins were absentee land-holders and did not stay here after the land was submerged. The Bhulias (weavers and shopkeepers) lost their contacts with the customers of the nearby villages and wanted to settle near the main road/town for their occupation; the Kansaris who were also absentee land owners shifted from Rampella. Some Khadias wanted to try their luck in land reclamation and agricultural labour in the would-be irrigated area and left the village. On the other hand, a few households of Majhians from a nearby village have moved to new Sapne to settle there permanently as they saw their future in fishing. The rest of the villagers decided to stay back hoping that the unsubmerged land of the village, however inferior and little it might be, would be distributed to them in future, and that the earnings from forest, fishing, and pasture would sustain them, and hence they neither wanted to move to resettlement colony nor to the old established villages. Their decision to settle in the periphery was also influenced by the persuasion of the government officers, and the poor of the nearby villages living on the same side of the river who had experienced a similar situation and had taken a similar decision. The few who left the village embarked on a new venture and did not move in with their relatives and friends. The village was fully acquired by the HLO even though part of the upland of the village did not actually get sub-merged (see Table 5.2). This is because some of the land belonged to the absentee Brahmins, Kansaris and Bhulias who wanted to move to the town; moreover the whole village and the best land were going to be sub-merged below RL 630. The villagers took a decision to shift to a new locality, about quarter of a km. away, so that they would be in a position to enjoy the unsubmerged land and the resources of the nearby forest and the reservoir. They did not want to shift to a completely new locality because their inadequate compensation would not have enabled them to purchase new land requiring reclamation and further investment.

People shifted to this new location in February 1956 and were given sites for houses and land for kitchen gardens as in other resettlement colonies. There was a plan outlay for roads and houses. The people were given the choice of staying as they liked but the habitation by caste/tribe-block has been evident, as in other colonies, and again people have encroached upon the roads and lanes used in the planned scheme. Since the distance was manageable people could

TABLE 5.2: Distribution of Resources in the Fully Sub-merged Village

Castes/ Tribes	No. of h.h	% to the total	Total Popln.	% to the total	Total land in 1925 (in acres)	Total Rayati land (in acres) 1980	Fore-shore lease (in acres) 1986	Land lease (in acres) 1986	Total land (in acres) 1986	Amt. of land per h.h (in acres)	Bullocks (in pairs)	Amt. of land per pair of bullocks (in acres)
Brahmin	LIVING NO MORE				154.83							
Kulta	IN THIS				0.47							
Kansari	VILLAGE				30.59							
Goud	3	6.82	20	9.57	3.31	4.70	5.71	1.00	11.41	3.80	5	2.82
Bhulia	1	2.27	5	2.39	34.22	0	2.52	0	2.52	2.52	1	2.52
Keut	2	4.45	5	2.39	20.26	2.05	1.32	0.30	3.67	1.84	2	1.84
Majhian	4	9.09	19	9.09	0	3.60	3.22	0.80	7.62	1.91	3	0.64
Ganda	15	34.09	64	30.62	39.32	15.64	23.96	2.70	42.30	2.82	11	3.85
Gond	15	34.09	68	32.54	138.41	9.24	14.58	1.85	26.67	1.78	12	2.22
Khadia	4	9.09	28	13.40	44.06	4.85	8.46	1.20	14.51	3.63	4	0.91
Total	44	100.00	209	100.00	465.47	40.08	59.77	7.85	108.70	2.47	38	2.86

shift all their belongings but initially stayed in huts which were easy to build as the required materials were locally available almost free-of-cost. Gradually they went on to construct permanent houses and are still doing so. During 1956-58, majority of the people (mostly Gandas) worked in digging of ponds/tanks, in transportation of the belongings of the oustees who had to move from the other side of the river in 1956 and in transportation of bamboos during 1956-73 (for about six months in a year mostly by the Gonds) from Barapahad jungle to the OPM along the river Ib. During the first year people used the compensation money for constructing their houses and buying food during periods of unemployment. People who had bullocks and labour force went on cultivating as much land as they could in 1956, and harvested reasonably well because the water of the reservoir did not touch RL 630. However, they suffered a heavy loss the next year when they cultivated more land with renewed vigour and the crops were sub-merged. In 1964, when people appealed to the Tahsildar about their poverty and the scarcity of agricultural land, he encouraged people to clear the earlier grazing land of the village and in 1974, the Tahsildar gave *patta* for about 40 acres of land. In the mean time, in 1960, people were also allotted the fore-shore lease and land lease as in the case of Pudhapara. However, the rate of lease is lower than that of Pudhapara and most of the land is land lease. For the first ten years, the production of the land lease land and the newly reclaimed land was very low, and people did not consider it to be an economic proposition, but they had to cultivate the land to be able to maintain a pair of bullocks for fear that without that the Revenue Deptt. would cancel their temporary lease. Even now most people manage for about three to four months from the net earnings of the land and for rest of the year they have to depend on other sources of livelihood. In such a situation there was necessarily a diversification of occupation among the people.

The richest man in the village is a Goud who had little land in the old village. He worked as a *mate* (supervisory assistant) to the Camp Officer when rehabilitation work and developmental work like digging of wells, tanks and ponds, and construction of an L.P. school were going on. He also worked as the caretaker of the oustees, on the other side of the river, when they dumped their belongings with him for further movement. It is alleged that he stole earthen tiles and useful/costly construction material of the oustees and that of the government for the construction of his own house. After sub-mergence there is extensive pasture as the water recedes during January-June and rest of the time the adjacent forest is available for grazing. People of the nearby villages, who do not have such facilities or who find it difficult or uneconomic to feed or take care of their cows and buffaloes, entrust people in such strategic locations to take care of their cattle. If a male calf is born it is taken by the donor, if a female calf is born it is kept by the caretaker, and the milk and the dung is used by the caretaker in lieu of his service. Depending on this system the Goud household had kept many buffaloes and cows and the herd grew later to 60 buffaloes and 55 calves. So he earned substantially from the sale of milk and dung and the output from his land went up because of the heavy use of dung. It is alleged that sometimes he used to sell the male calves of others since it was difficult for the donor to ascertain it in such a herd (*goth*). Gradually he amassed wealth by lending money and paddy to the villagers and sometimes selling the pawned items forfeited by the borrowers. He also got a sale deed signed by a dying Bhulia for 2.73 acres of land, who had borrowed Rs. 300 in 1965 and needed some more money for his family to meet medical expenses. He continued to harvest the crops of the land for 20 years when the now-grown-up son of the Bhulia requested the villagers to help him. Since the villagers were already agitated against him, they helped the Bhulia in appealing to the High Court to obtain a stay order saying that the Goud could not harvest from that land until the case is finally decided. The Goud went on cultivating the land and the villagers have been reaping the paddy, about 21 qtls., during 1985-87, and utilising part of the harvest for the construction of the Bhagabat temple and giving the rest to the Bhulia. It is alleged by the Goud that the villagers used sorcery to kill his vast stock of cattle and now he has just 8 buffaloes and 5 calves. The Goud visited the District Veterinary Surgeon at Sambalpur and Cuttack but they could not save the cattle from dying. The Goud and his relatives have been leading a miserable life since nobody talks to them, no labourer of the village works for them, their houses were stoned several times at night, their cash and jewellery were stolen by thieves, the local Chamars were not allowed to lift their dead cattle and they were virtually ex-communicated. The Chairman of the Panchayat Samiti, Shatrughna Panda, who is very influential in this locality and who has been in this post from the beginning, came to his rescue, and the Gouds have been able to stay in the village but the litigation continues. It has been necessary to discuss the history of the

Goud households because their activities unified the rest of the village.

The Bhulia household has a small shop, the only one in the village, and the male head also manages agriculture and fishing on a shared basis. The rest of the villagers manage by fishing, agriculture, labour, sale of forest produce at Rengali and Sambalpur, milk and cowdung, etc. The forest produce includes edible leaves, roots, flowers and fruits, bamboo shoots, honey, gums of different trees and occasionally birds and mushrooms and also firewood, timber, leaves for pots, and tooth brush. Villagers, mostly the Gandas, used to sell the smaller items almost regularly at Rengali and Sambalpur by shuttling in local trains. Sometimes they slept overnight at Sambalpur to sell these goods. They also sold heavier and bigger/costlier goods at Rengali and sometimes at Sambalpur. It was rather difficult to reach Sambalpur because they had to pass through many forest check-gates and the people did not know the gate-keepers intimately. Sometimes the gate-keepers did not accept bribes especially when their senior officers were on duty, and filed cases against them after seizing the forest produce. Since 1985, people have stopped going to Rengali and Sambalpur with the more expensive goods because the checking has been intensified and the people are afraid of fines that are beyond their capacity to pay. The villagers graze their cattle in the jungle by paying a nominal commutation fee and are allowed to collect firewood and timber for domestic use by paying the necessary license fees. At this time they can collect more than their due by bribing the lower forest officials. However, they are heavily penalised if they are caught while taking out firewood or timber by boat for selling outside along or across the river. But surprisingly the services of villagers are used for similar work when the forest officials are bribed by wealthy and influential people of the neighbouring/ distant villages to take these items in bulk. The villagers provide the labour for which they are paid and they also get a share in the bribe, which they use for collective purposes. They are also entrusted to keep the goods including the boats seized by the forest guards and act as witnesses in cases of theft. Further, they work as informers to forest officials when they know about a possible plan for theft or actual theft of the forest goods by 'outsiders'. The strategic location of the village enables the people to collaborate with the forest officers in such malpractices to cheat the State of its dues. The recent decision of the government to let loose two tigers in the open forest has somehow dissuaded the 'weaker ones' to go to the forest for the collection of produce. This has also deterred the herdsboys from taking the cattle to the interior parts of the jungle. But it would not have any effect on large scale theft since it is an organised activity involving a large number of people.

Probably, the most important occupation in this village is fishing and related activities like supplying and selling of fish. Depending on the season, the level of water in the reservoir, and the available man-power, people use different types of boats and nets to catch fish of different sizes and varieties. They also fish in their paddy fields during rainy season mostly with small fishing implements made of bamboo, which is locally available. People know their make and also the boat which is made of locally available wood. There are 18 boats in the village out of which 12 boats have been financed by the SBI in 1980 and one boat by the PACS in 1986. People who do not own boats offer their labour to the boat owner and take a share in the catch — the catch is divided, one share goes to the boat, one to the net and one share each to every person, irrespective of the work done by them. There are two Gandas who buy fish from the fisherman and sell it to the dealers at Rengali who in turn keep it in ice and send it to Rourkela and Tatanagar. The petty traders get a commission of Re.0.50 per kg.; they also make a profit by selling the fish which is the difference in weight while purchasing and selling. These petty traders sometimes arrange for the weekly ration and other small needs of the fishermen from some fish traders and or Marwaris of Rengali. Some-times they pay between Rs. 100 to Rs. 200 as 'attachment fee' to the fishermen so that they would sell all their fish (except for their own consumption and on rare occasions) to them for a year; this amount may be adjusted in the payment to the fisherman or it may be waived as such. The fishermen are being exploited by the traders and petty traders/middlemen and because of such attachment they cannot have any say in the disposal/marketing of the catch. The fishermen are also cheated in weights and rates while buying groceries from the agent of the trader or the trader himself. The fishermen pay Rs. 50 per head as fishing tax and if they do not have a fishing license their boat and net could be seized by the Fishery officials. Despite some of the facilities provided by the formal financial agencies — unlike Pudhapara where most of the applicants were refused assistance from such agencies — the people who depend on fishing are not in a position to pay the instalments in time and many of them are already defaulters. Hence, some people build their own boat and net and apply for a loan in cash and hence they are not being financed by the formal agencies which usually provide the boat and the net worth Rs. 4,000 per fisherman. The cheaper/easy availability of boats in this village has led some people to use boats for stealing valuable forest produce to sell it elsewhere and hence they have been penalised when caught by the forest officials.

Agriculture is not an economic proposition in this village. The left over land is not that productive and the *mutkel* soil around the village is full of pebbles and has little water holding capacity and hence there is no chance of growing any vegetables in the kitchen gardens. The crops, in general, are also destroyed by wild animals if not guarded properly at the time of maturing. Unlike Pudhapara there is no summer paddy. Because of the special terrain water does not recede until February and does not allow the cultivation of summer paddy. No one except the Gouds employ agricultural labour. The people work as agricultural labourers in the nearby villages in rainy season when they do not have much stock of grains of their own, when they are not in a position to fish, or go to forest for collection, and when they really need wages in kind. But unlike Pudhapara these people are not in a position to continue for a long period because of the distance of the village from the main road. Two Gonds and eight Gandas were working in the rice mill at Rengali for a long time but when mechanisation was introduced and they were asked to report for night shifts they hesitated, and stopped the work completely in 1980 when somebody met with a fatal accident in the mill. The poor returns from agriculture, the 'non-availability' of agricultural and non-agricultural wage labour, because of the location of the village, and the severe decrease in earnings from forest resources since 1985 have compelled the people to depend upon fishing and bidi making, the earnings from which naturally increase if there are more hands in the family, at least temporarily. Only one to two households in each caste/tribe of the village are slowly coming up because of multiple sources of income, hard labour, and minimal expenditure. But overall the pauperisation of the villagers, which started during the Brahmins' exploitation in the old village, is still continuing albeit with a difference. Nobody has passed class 8th in this village; the consumption pattern of the families and the dilapidated houses of most of the people reveal their poverty even though they are consuming less liquor than before.

Comparison

Before the construction of the Hirakud dam, and the sub-mergence of land, the two villages were encapsulated in the same regional economy. Although the fully submerged village Sapne had witnessed the pauperisation of the peasantry to a greater extent than the partly submerged village Pudhapara, people in both the villages have undergone a lot of hardship because the sources of livelihood for the peasants were virtually cut off. People in Pudhapara have been able to revive their past to some extent because of the non-submergence of their houses, its nearness to industrial-urban centres and hence access to several non-agricultural sources of income, and also due to the availability of more land lease and fore-shore lease land compared to Sapne. In both the villages, bidi-making, fishing and related activities have become important irrespective of castes. People of the fully submerged village suffered more than the people of the partly submerged village because of lack of initial resources, poor location and the complete absence of leadership. The nefarious activities of the Goud household, in Sapne, compelled the rest of the villagers to unite. On the other hand, Pudhapara is a highly faction-ridden village; the bone of contention being cultivation of the summer crop and ownership of submergible lease land. The competition is so stiff that native villagers who came back to the village after shifting to some other localities were not welcomed. It is anticipated that people in Sapne would find it difficult to survive if forest rules are strictly implemented, and the fishermen are not liberally financed. People in Pudhapara would have to struggle hard if government does not allow them the cultivation of submergible land which necessarily leads to the silting of the reservoir. In the ultimate analysis the dam and submerging seem to have done them more harm than good (Baboo, 1991(c): 287-306).

NOTES

1. The development of such a flood-drought resistant variety of paddy, through research, would be very beneficial to people in the off-shore villages.
2. For a long time *Samalai Puja* is being performed in this village with a lot of pomp and grandeur. On this occasion each caste-ward of this village offers a goat when the idol of the deity is taken around the village. In 1982, instigated by a few notorious people, the Gandas arranged a goat and other items of worship to offer to the deity at their own ward. However, these notorious people

did not support the Gandas when the rest of the villagers did not want to accept the offerings of the Gandas. The Gandas felt humiliated and tried to cut off relation with the villagers as far as possible. In the mean time, one of the wicked and arrogant Telis raped a woman of a wanderer group, who were living in the outskirts of the village. A few members of the group had altercations with the Telis but the Telis threatened them with dire consequences. Being enraged the whole group of the wanderers came to the village one day and ran amuck with spears and sticks in their hands. No one from the village could get out of the house; the villagers felt threatened and consequently accused the Telis for this misfortune. Later the Police came and sorted out the matter. Now the Telis, who were very poor and have prospered very fast due to illegal practice and due to regular income from blue-collar works. Then support the Gandas because the Gandas do not get along with the rest of the villagers. The Gandas have felt so discriminated that now they have constructed their own *Bhagabat Temple* and conduct their own *Nam Yajna*. The village is faction-ridden and their is none whom all the villagers pay respect in the matter of critical decisions.

6

REHABILITATION OF THE OUSTEES IN SETTLED VILLAGES

Introduction

Oustees, who did not go to the camps and resettlement colonies nor stayed in the peripheral villages/nearby locales went to settle in already settled villages or towns. It was expected that, given the option, as a rule, people would like to settle in area similar to their own social and physical environment, and where they would get employment suiting to their skills and capabilities. However, taking the economic rationale into consideration it might be argued that the tendency of people, regarding resettlement, would decrease from sub-urban wet village to tribal dry village on the two extremes. In this section we would see the processes of their resettlement in the six types of villages that we have suggested earlier. For the purpose of comparison in terms of spatio-cultural categories, we have arranged them in three settings.

(A) The Tribal Setting

The two tribal villages — one dry and the other wet — are situated in Attabira Block of Sambalpur district, about eight km. apart. Before the introduction of irrigation from the Bargarh canal system of the Hirakud dam the two villages were encapsulated in similar types of socio-economic fabric. The tribal dry village (TDV) is close to the Barapahar forests, and is five km. away from the canal and the nearest bus-stop. The tribal wet village (TWV) is close to the canal and the bus-stop and the present forest (after the depletion) is eight km. away. The TWV has received oustees, mostly tribals, whereas the oustees are mostly non-tribals in the TDV. In 1987, the position of the oustees in these two villages is as follows :

TABLE 6.1: Distribution of Oustees in the TDV and the TWV

Caste/ Tribe	No. of households	Population	Caste/ Tribe	No. of households	Population
	TDV			*TWV*	
Goud	2	11	Kulta	2	24
Keut	6	41	Sahara	3	5
Kandha	1	8	Mirdha	9	66
Gond	3	14	Khadia	3	17
Total	12	74		17	112

From Tables 6.1, 6.2 and 6.3, it is clear that in the TDV they constitute 18.75 per cent of the households and 24.67 per cent of the population and in the TWV they constitute 17 per cent of the households and 20.29 per cent of the population. Further, the percentage of the tribal oustees to the total oustees in these TDV and TWV is 29.73 per cent and 78.57 per cent respectively. In the TDV all the oustees, except the Keuts, are residing in a separate ward (*para*) at a distance from the main settlement (*basti*) whereas in the TWV they reside inside the main village. In both the villages the corresponding castes/tribes were already living there. Even though these two villages were already settled for at least 100 years, as the records and old people suggest, all the private land of the villages were not as yet cultivated because of dependence on forest and fast growth of shrubs on the land which is cleared. The purchasing of land by the oustees in both the villages, the reclamation of land primarily by the newly habitated Oraon and Khadia in the TDV, and the irrigation facilities in the TWV has led to increasing pressure on land, although not with similar results in both the villages. Further, when land is prohibitively costly in the TWV, it is rather very cheap in the TDV, more so because forest rather than land is the main source of living in the TDV and agriculture does not seem to be an economic proposition, too.

Rehabilitation in the TDV

The oustees into the TDV were invited by a relative/acquaintance, or had some link in terms of business, or came there because of easy

TABLE 6.2: Distribution of Resources in the TDV

Tribes/ Castes	No. of h.h.	% to the total	Total Popln.	% to the total	Amt. of land (in acres) 1926	Amt. of land (in acres) 1987	Amt. of land per h.h. (in acres)	Pair of Bullocks	Amt. of land per pair of bullocks (in acres)	No. of h.h of oustees	Population of oustees
Binjhal	7	10.94	26	8.67	39.50	50.16	7.17	3	16.72	0	0
Gond	21	32.81	92	30.67	48.15	55.99	2.67	11	5.09	3	14
Oraon	8	12.50	41	13.67	0	0	0	6	—	0	0
Khadia	2	3.13	9	3.00	0	0	0	2	—	0	0
Kandha	6	9.38	25	8.33	0	0	0	1	—	1	8
Kulta	5	7.81	24	8.00	73.04	95.89	9.18	5	19.18	0	0
Goud	4	6.25	16	5.33	0	0	0	3	—	2	11
Kumbhar	2	3.13	11	3.67	0	0	0	2	—	0	0
Keut	8	12.50	46	15.33	4.68	7.93	0.99	3	2.64	6	41
Ghasia	1	1.56	10	3.33	2.70	2.90	2.90	0	—	0	0
Total	64	100.01	300	100.00	168.07	212.87	3.33	36	5.91	12	74

TABLE 6.3: Distribution of Resources in the TWV

Tribes/ Castes	No. of h.h.	% to the total	Total Popln.	% to the total	Amt. of land (in acres) 1926	Amt. of land (in acres) 1987	Amt. of land per h.h. (in acres)	Pair of Bullocks & Buffaloes	Amt. of land per pair of bullocks (in acres)	No. of h.h of oustees	Population of oustees
Sahara	33	33	152	27.54	186.48	76.25	2.31	12 + 5	4.49	3	5
Munda	14	14	84	15.22	3.85	2.98	0.40	6 + 7	0.43	0	0
Mirdha	10	10	73	13.22	0	25.50	2.55	4 + 12	1.59	9	66
Binjal	1	1	6	1.09	0	0	0	0	0	0	0
Khadia	6	6	31	5.62	0	0	0	1 + 0	—	3	17
Kulta	15	15	106	19.20	64.75	134.61	8.97	6 + 15	6.41	2	24
Bhat	3	3	15	2.72	0	2.00C	0.67	1 + 0	2.00	0	0
Keut	1	1	3	0.54	0	2.00C	2.00	0 + 1	2.00	0	0
Satnami	4	4	18	3.26	0	0	0	2 + 0	—	0	0
Telugu	10	10	48	8.70	0	27.45	2.75	8 + 4	2.29	0	0
Goud	3	3	16	2.90	0	0	—	0 + 1	—	0	0
Total	100	100	552	100.01	255.08	291.82	2.92	40 + 45*	3.43	17	112

Notes: 1. * refers to pair of buffaloes.
2. C refers to ceiling surplus land.

and cheap availability of land and ready-made house, and the habitation of their own caste/tribe. All of them, without exception, told that nearness to forest would enable them to get firewood, construction material for the house and implements, edibles from the forest virtually free; and they hoped that in case of failure of crops they could sell the forest produce in the nearby villages. All these oustees also came from different neighbouring villages on the other side of the Barapahar forest. In their old villages the Keuts managed through fishing, parched rice selling and agriculture; the Gouds from agriculture, cattle herding and selling of milk and dung; and the Kandhas and Gonds from agriculture and agricultural labour. In 1956, these people were brought here by trucks and all of them, except two households of Keut, lived in a separate ward by purchasing land from the Kulta Gountia at a very nominal price.

Initially, all of them were given shelter by their acquaintances and kinsmen, or came straight into a purchased house, as in the case of two households of Keut. Then they constructed their huts by *daro* (dried branches), bamboo, clay and straw, all of which were locally available. The villagers gave them some bundles of straw or they bought it from the neighbouring villages. Gradually, they constructed their own houses in the Talipara, a place about 300 metres from the main *basti* (housing settlement). They could not buy good agricultural land because such land was scarce, and the people who had such land (the Kulta Gountia) had no need to sell it (see Table 6.2). They purchased about four acres of land in this village and eight acres of land in a neighbouring village but these plots of land were not being regularly cultivated by the owners. Hence, the oustees had to work very hard to make them cultivable. Two of the oustees found lots of difficulties in getting *patta* (record of rights) because they had bought land from the Scheduled Tribes. Ignorance of law cost them heavily since the sellers of the land took possession of the already sold land when the Orissa Land Reform (OLR) Act, 19/1975 was introduced whereby lands, on usufructuary mortgage for more than seven years became automatically free. The oustees could also reclaim very little government land because they were discouraged from doing so. They did not have the initial capital to do so by labourers, nor could they spend time later when they exhausted their compensation in conspicuous consumption. Some of them also did not keep well in the new environment, could not cope with the dependence on forest, and had to spend on health care. The construction of canal increased the distance between some villages, on the other side of the canal, and the forest; cultivation of summer paddy also led to the extinction of some trees, especially mango and mahua, from the fields of the people in the irrigated area; and hence they depended increasingly on people of the TDV for firewood, leaves for pots, tooth brush, jungle fruits, roots and off-shoots and also timber for construction of houses. All the households, including all the oustees, but excluding the Kultas, have been surviving on such 'illegal' collection from the forest, limited agricultural labour in nearby villages and bamboo cutting for the OPM, etc. The produce from their land meets their consumption need for three to four months in a normal year.

Their hand-to-mouth existence and drinking habits compel them to borrow from Gaji Pathan of Paharsirgida village, about 10 km. away, at a usurious rate of interest, which works out to be around 420 per cent per annum, resulting in a debt-trap from which they find it difficult to extricate themselves. They have been pauperised to such an extent that they pawned all their tangible items like ornaments and utensils, and have forfeited those later on. Their determination to get rid of the vicious cycle of borrowing-repaying-borrowing has landed them into transactions with slightly lesser exploitative and oppressive agents like the village school teacher and the local moneylenders, but not completely out of usury. The question is if there is no collusion between them and the forest officials for the sale of forest produce, and if there is strict checking, how will they survive? Only one household of the oustees, who purchased agricultural land and a ready-made house in this village to start with, and gave lower shares to his brothers and who is also a hard-working, jack-of-all trades person has come up really well primarily because he had considerable wealth in the old village and had utilised the compensation and his own stock intelligently.

As regards the social domain inside the village, the oustees faced lot of problems in interaction and adjustment since they came from big multi-caste villages to reside in a small one. They introduced *Ratha Yatra* (Car Festival) and *Nam Yajna* and performed in the Talipara and after two years shifted to the Uparpara because the Gountia family lived there. Since they had to walk a long distance for collecting water from the pond and found it difficult in summer, they requested the Gountia for a plot of land to dig a pond on their own with some help from the villagers. The Gountia did not give them the plot they desired but gave them a plot where they could not get water after digging a lot. So they were dissatisfied. There were several other reasons for their dissatisfaction. Gradually they got alienated from the old inhabitants of the village. It was alleged that the oustees had received a lot of compensation money — none had got more than Rs. 2,500 — with which they bought some land and squandered the rest on chicken, liquor, etc. This was envied by the people of the village. They came to the village meetings drunk and did not respect the native inhabitants. On trifle matters they flaunted their wealth and threatened litigation and did not calm down. On the other hand, the oustees alleged that they were rarely called to the village meetings; even when called, their opinions were never respected; that the village fund was increasingly being used for facilities primarily available to the Uparpara, e.g., pond, Lower Primary School, Bhagabat temple etc. They further alleged that nobody from their ward was ever made a ward member; that the Kultas in the Uparpara were very arrogant in their behaviour; that they were not allowed to be associated in the *Kado-jatra* and *Khar Pujei* festivals and had to offer separate sacrifice-animals, and the Jhankar was also asked not to cooperate with them. The Kulta Gountia asked them to provide collective unpaid labour for repairing common embankment but did not allow the much needed water to flow below his plots unto the oustees'; that their names were not included in different developmental activities of the government; that the old inhabitants of the village did not allow them to reclaim the land, and in case of argument humiliated them by referring to their oustee status. The feeling has been sharpened in recent times and the younger generation has been very vocal; they have stopped performing the *Ratha Yatra* and the *Nam Yajna* and have constructed a separate Bhagabat temple from contribution of money, labour and collection of timbers from the nearby forest.

It is rather surprising that even though the oustees had some acquaintances in this village and were helped initially and still share a feeling of belonging to the same village, their relationship between them and the villagers has never been very cordial. All these factors show that the habitation of most of the oustees in a separate ward at a distance from the natives' settlement and the absence of most of the villagers, from the village, in the day time — for going to the forest — restricted interaction between the 'insiders' and the 'oustees'. This and their different background inhibited social interaction and hampered the process of assimilation.

Rehabilitation in the TWV

The oustees settled in the TWV, except the Khadias, came from big villages and were also very well-off. The Khadias came from the fully sub-merged village Sapne, and came here after staying in two other villages where they stayed for five years and eight years respectively. They did not get any compensation because their mother, in their absence, told the authorities that three of her sons were already dead, and gave all the money to only one of her sons. These Khadias went on doing agricultural labour and soil digging in two villages and were given one acre of land by the local Zamindar, for personal cultivation, in lieu of their devoted services. These Khadias have been surviving on 'stealing' of forest produce, soil digging and agricultural labour. They have temporary houses constructed on government grazing land, as they did in the two other villages in which they settled earlier. It might be said that these people were not yet rehabilitated and because of 'landlessness' did not feel themselves as a part of the village community (see Table 6.3). They were also not considered as potential threat to the villagers; rather their service was very much required in a labour scarce double-cropped village.

Two of the Sahara households are headed by two childless widows who are sisters and more than seventy years old. They have relatives in this village who are now waiting for the death of these two women so that they can inherit their property. They got Rs. 2,500 as compensation and purchased six acres of rain-fed land in nearby villages which were within five km. from the TWV because suitable land was not available in the village. They managed by cultivating the land, agricultural labour and sometimes on the sale of forest produce. For the last twenty years, they have been leasing out their land because of its distance from the TWV, sickness and subsequent death of their husbands, and their own inability to look after and arrange for cultivation. Both of them had pawned their ornaments to meet contingent expenditure and later forfeited them. After the death of their husbands, they survived on the sale of parched rice and minor forest produce, and paddy from the leased out land. Now that they are too old to engage in any activity requiring strenuous physical labour, they are surviving with lot of difficulties, relying solely on the lease of their land; so much so that they find it difficult even to repair their dilapidated houses. The other Sahara who was with his in-laws, at the time of compensation was cheated by his brother who took advantage of his absence. He did not get any compensation although his father had ten acres of land, because he was reported dead by his brothers. Before settling down in the TWV he lived in five different villages, for a total period of 14 years working as attached labourer and in the mean time five of his children died. He wanted to give his son education by working as an attached labourer but was not successful. He also earned from the sale of forest produce, and for the last few years his wife has been selling vegetables, rice and dried fish, etc., from village to village, primarily because the man is now not in a position to do hard labour as he is suffering from filaria.

One of the Kultas had his father-in-law in this village who helped him to purchase land and gave him temporary accommodation. Later when the man gradually began to prosper through hard labour his brothers-in-law started envying him and the relationship between them got strained. The man died in 1971 but his three sons — who are all married — worked very hard on land reclamation, leasing in and mortgaging in land, agricultural labour, selling of rice, transportation in carts, collection of mahua, etc. and are now constructing a big cement building worth about Rs. 1.5 lakhs. Initially, they suffered a lot when the three children were small and the land was scarcely productive and non-irrigated. On the other hand the other Kulta household, which has been staying here for the last 6 years, stayed in two other villages. His grand-father had 52 acres of land in the old village and got Rs. 13,500 as compensation. They were notified to get Rs. 6,700 as compensation for the house but received only Rs. 3,500 because the absentee Gountia was to get Rs. 5,000 and the latter did not want any tenant to get more than him; he asked the concerned officers to undervalue his house. This is an example of Gountias calling the tune at the time of compensation. Sometimes they took 25 per cent of the compensation saying that it was *nazarana* (tribute) and also claimed compensation for tanks, ponds, etc. These Kultas went around looking for land and at long last purchased 45 acres of land from a goldsmith for Rs. 20,000. Even after payment of Rs. 19,000 and cultivation of the land for a few years the goldsmith delayed the registration of the land and finally denied taking the money. A simple handnote however, came to the rescue of the Kultas and the land was finally registered after 7 years. In the mean time, there was a lot of legal expenditure, and the father-in-law of the man, who was the primary shareholder in the transaction of the land, died and his sons did not respect their brother-in-law and he was given only 9 acres of inferior land for his Rs. 9,500 on the ground that he had not paid for the legal expenditure. Since he did not have good relationship with them and had taken to litigation against them he left the village, out of fear, for another village and there cultivated some land on lease for 10 years. He also bought some land from a tribal which could not be registered and consequently lost the money. Later he bought three acres of rainfed land for Rs. 3,600 which could be irrigated — after a lot of labour and expenditure. In the mean time, he incurred a lot of expenditure on the marriage of his sons, daughters and grand-daughters; litigation, shifting, etc. Now his is a shattered family surviving on agriculture, dairy farming, and a moving sweet-meat shop. One of his sons has become a vagabond and there is no peace in the family.

Nine out of the ten households of Mirdhas came from two villages, Baghabahali-Resham and Malda, and are related by kinship. Eight of the households came together in 1956 and one household, that had shifted twice, came here in 1973. The Mirdhas were very well-off in their old villages but most of the houses were ravaged by accidental fire the year they left; so they got very little compensation for the houses. For two years they went on looking for land in places hundreds of kilometres away but could not get sufficient and suitable land at a reasonable price; if suitable land was found no proper house-site was available or the villagers dissuaded them from settling there, and so on. Finally, they purchased 25 acres of land for Rs. 5,050 from an absentee of this TWV and divided it amongst them. Part of this land was already being cultivated by the Kultas of this village because the land owner was not staying there; they wanted to cultivate the land even when the Mirdhas had purchased it and consequently there was some dispute. The Kultas were very envious of the Mirdhas because they purchased a big chunk of land, and brought about two hundred heads of cattle, and two truck loads of paddy with them. The Kultas did not allow the Mirdhas to take out their cattle from the main gate of their houses; sprayed rumour that a Mirdha had illicit relation with a Sahara woman — to discredit them; the villagers were warned by the Kultas not to have any social relation with the Mirdhas and they were discriminated against in every social sphere. Due to non-availability of water and long grass, eighty per cent of the cattle of the Mirdhas died within two years. Sometimes the cattle were also stolen and sold outside the village. The Mirdhas went on reclaiming their land resting for about 4 hours in the night.

They worked on moonlit nights. They worked in canal digging, transporting of timber and stone, etc. to earn some money; gradually constructed the houses and finally made the land cultivable. They reclaimed part of the land, cultivated that portion and invested the output in other productive activities. For four years they lived very miserly, gave of drinking completely, and now four of the nine households are well-off. Others could not come up because of late entry into the village, large family with small children, inability to cut down on drinking and lethargy.

So, as in the TDV here also the oustees had to face a lot of difficulties and until now one can observe some sort of distantiation between the 'insiders' and the 'oustees'. It also shows that only a few among the well-off Kultas, Mirdhas, and Saharas have been able to revive their past albeit with lot of difficulties; in general they have declined in the economic ladder. It may also be noted that in their old villages they raised one crop of paddy, enjoyed life with community feeling, observed cultural and religious functions, and there was no rat-race. There was a complete change in their lifestyle when they moved to the TWV.

Comparison and Conclusion

It should be noted here that since the oustees constituted 20 per cent to 25 per cent in both the villages they were necessarily a minority and started very much as underdogs. Over years of struggle some of them have come up in the economic ladder and some of them have become important in the village primarily because of their wealth. On the other hand, the rest of them could not outgrow their oustee status and people identify them as *budi anchalar loka* (reservoir oustees). This has remained as a stigma with them. One important difference between these two villages is that the TWV had some distinct advantages over the TDV in terms of location, accessibility, education and health facilities, potable water, economic opportunities, and most importantly canal irrigation facilities. Consequently, the life-styles of the oustees in these two villages show some differences. In the TDV they are primarily depending on forest and are at the mercy of the forest officials; they also have to toil a lot and move out of the village almost regularly to eke out a living, which they did not have to do in their old villages. On the other hand, in the TWV, the oustees got better opportunities to reconstruct their economic past. However, in both the villages they have lost contact with their relatives and friends and have sometimes found it difficult to arrange marriages for the children. The Mirdhas in the TWV were related to each other by affinal and kinship ties and were in a better position to withstand the hardships of the initial days. Along with the introduction of summer crop and profitable market gardening, they are prospering and feeling some satisfaction for the sacrifices they made for the construction of the dam. People in the TDV are, however, counting their days. They summarised their plight in one sentence : "*redi chaluthibar tak thundi chaluchhe*", i.e., "we can survive as long as we are able to move around and work; the day we cease to work we will have nothing to eat". Whereas rehabilitation in the wet village has allowed the oustees to have something to show, it is not so in the TDV. But it must be kept in mind that in the latter the oustees started with poor initial resources. At a social level, since the oustees came to settle in tribal village and since many of them were tribals they were not tied that much by jajmani network and hence no problem in this regard, but the Mirdhas' traditional unwillingness to accept water from any other caste or tribal groups led to some problem in the Kulta dominated village. From the policy point of view it gives us the lesson that adjustment becomes easier and economic hardship can be mitigated if there is block rehabilitation of people in terms of relatives and villages. Further, if there is proper economic rehabilitation then people might tend to forget the social costs (Baboo, 1991 (b): 16-30).

(B) Rehabilitation in the Peasant Villages

As regards rehabilitation, it was really difficult to select the peasant villages, far from the forest, because the price of land is usually cheaper near the forests — and many of them are likely to be tribal villages — where the oustees might be in a position to purchase land. Further, it was not possible to select both the villages in the same Block. It might be noted that by coincidence or because of cheapness of land most of the scattered oustees have settled in the villages adjacent to forest or Zamindaris where large chunk of land was available for purchase. It was not so in multi-caste villages in the plains where most of the land was already under cultivation and available with people who did not feel the urgency to sell. Large chunks of land was sold sometimes by absentees who stayed in another nearby village or who had taken to occupations other than agriculture. The Gountias/Zamindars who did not like to retain their relatively unproductive and distant plots of land after the abolition of the Gounti/Zamindari systems in 1951, and who faced labour scarcity when people went to work in canal construction and later for industrial/non-agricultural work also sold land.

Ultimately, the two villages were selected in Bargarh sub-division : the peasant dry village (PDV) in Bhatli Block and the peasant wet village (PWV) in Attabira Block. Both are multi-caste big villages with almost comparable castes/tribes and in both the villages the SC/ST population is substantial. In the PDV only the Kultas and the Gandas have resettled and that too they have come mostly from one village each. On the other hand, in the PWV people from five castes and Sahara tribe have come but the contribution of the oustees to the total population in the PDV and the PWV is 8 per cent and 20 per cent, respectively (see Table 6.4 and Table 6.5).

Rehabilitation in the PDV

In the PDV, the Kultas came from Ghenachal, Kenapali and Rebo. They came here because of some relatives and acquaintances and where people of their own castes were in majority. Land was also available, for sale, in plenty and in reasonable price because the absentee Gountia and absentee Marwaris wanted to sell their land. All the Kulta oustees have settled enblock at one end of the village close to the Luhura and the Ganda settlements and not inside the village because no space was available. Initially, they were helped by local Kultas, especially for accommodation. Gradually disputes started because the natives called their oustee status; did not return the cash/paddy they had borrowed from them; planned theft from their houses; did not allow them to encroach on the grazing land for cultivation of groundnut, gram, etc.; did not allow the water from their fields to flow on to the oustees' fields through a separate channel for irrigation during the drought period, and discriminated them in terms of governmental help/subsidy available to the villagers by not incorporating their names in the list of beneficiaries. This is also true for the Ganda oustees resettling in the village. The difficulty was so unsurmountable that one household of Kulta who had some resources, sold his property and left this village for a double-cropped village after staying here for 10 years. The two households of Kultas

TABLE 6.4: Distribution of Resources in the PDV

Castes/ Tribes	No. of h.h.	% to the total	Total Popln.	% to the total	Amt. of land (in acres) 1926	Amt. of land (in acres) 1987	Amt. of land per h.h (in acres)	Pair of Bullocks	Amt. of land per pair of bullocks (in acres)	No. of h.h. of oustees	Population of oustees
Brahmin	1	0.48	11	1.17	0	2.89	2.89	0	—	0	0
Kulta	91	43.97	464	49.52	183.89	457.73	5.03	8+71	5.79	14	61
Goud	12	5.80	44	4.70	1.10	17.60	1.47	5	3.52	0	0
Teli	10	4.83	49	5.23	0	40.30	4.03	8	5.04	0	0
Bhulia	4	1.93	20	2.13	0	0	0	0	0	0	0
Keut	3	1.44	10	1.07	49.97	4.87	1.62	2	2.44	0	0
Dhuba	2	0.97	4	0.43	0	0	0	1	—	0	0
Bhandari	2	0.97	10	1.07	0	4.06	2.03	0	—	0	0
Ghantra	18	8.70	71	7.58	0	7.44	0.41	6	1.24	0	0
Pap	5	2.42	17	1.81	0	3.00	0.60	2	1.50	0	0
Ganda	21	10.14	76	8.11	21.93	4.14	0.20	12	0.35	4	14
Ghasia	10	4.83	40	4.27	0	0	0	2	—	0	0
Sahara	22	10.63	86	9.18	155.14	23.72	1.08	2+8	2.37	0	0
Gond	3	1.44	16	1.71	66.11	25.74	8.58	1	25.74	0	0
Binjhal	3	1.44	19	2.03	0	3.37	1.12	2	1.69	0	0
Total	207	99.99	937	100.01	691.66	686.52	3.32	10* +120	5.28	18	75

Note: * Refers to pair of buffaloes.

TABLE 6.5: Distribution of Resources in the PWV

Castes/ Tribes	No. of h.h	% to the total	Total Popln.	% to the total	Amt. of total land (in acres) 1926	Amt. of total land (in acres) 1987	Amt. of land per h.h (in acres)	Pair of Bullocks	Amt. of land per pair of bullocks (in acres)	No. of h.h of oustees	Population of oustees
Brahmin	0	0	0	0	80.34	57.74	absentee	0	0	0	0
Gosein	1	0.50	7	0.71	0.07	4.56	4.56	1	4.56	0	0
Kulta	69	34.50	406	40.93	183.42	215.42	3.12	16+46	3.47	10	59
Mali	2	1.00	8	0.81	3.15	4.14	2.07	1	4.14	0	0
Goud	2	1.00	15	1.51	16.44	10.72	5.36	1	10.72	0	0
Teli	3	1.50	20	2.02	5.45	6.00	2.00	1	6.00	0	0
Keut	7	3.50	27	2.72	6.77	11.74	1.68	3	3.91	3	7
Dumbal	3	1.50	12	1.21	26.65	5.95	1.98	1+0	5.95	6	28
Dhuba	6	3.00	31	3.13	0	0.54	0.09	1+3	0.13	1	4
Bhandari	4	2.00	23	2.32	0	3.61	0.90	2+0	1.80	0	0
Telugu	1	0.50	3	0.30	0	16.00	16.00	1	16.00	0	0
Ganda	23	11.50	108	10.89	4.82	5.53	0.24	1+7	0.79	6	18
Chamar	27	13.50	106	10.69	16.29	13.56	0.52	13	1.04	0	0
Mirdha	1	0.50	7	0.71	0	1.64	1.64	0	—	1	7
Gond	1	0.50	5	0.50	0	0	0	1	—	0	0
Sahara	50	25.00	214	21.57	58.46	44.97	0.90	1+16	2.64	15	66
Total	200	100.00	992	100.02	401.86	402.12	2.01	22* + 95	3.44**	42	189

Notes: * Refers to pair of buffaloes.

** The Kultas have three tractors and hence own less pairs of bullocks.

who are from Rebo, Madhya Pradesh, have been envied by the rich Telis who went on to the extent of dismantling the cement tubes and other construction materials of a proposed lift point that would have benefited the oustees directly and lessened their dependence on the Telis, for irrigation.

All the Kultas, who came to settle in this village, have purchased some land with the compensation they had received. None of them went for purchasing gold and other intangible items because they usually had some gold at home. Their investment was in construction of good house, good bullocks, and purchase and reclamation of land. They cut down their consumption to the minimum to save something for the rainy days. All of them, except one household, had land in their old village. All the Kulta households lease in land and only one household has been able to revive its earlier economic status primarily because of small family, miserly habits and profit from petty-trading in rice; rest of them are still struggling. To begin with, all the households except one, who is an ex-Gountia, worked on road construction, railway lines, stone crushing, transportation of boulders, and selling of firewood and timbers up to 1963-64, at Bargarh, 20 km. away. Two households are still working as supervisory assistants to the Marwaris at Bhatli with a monthly salary of Rs. 450 each and helping in various odd jobs such as supervision of store rooms and domestic works, selling of different items and measuring of *mahua*, etc. One of them is supplementing his earning from carpentry and two of them were engaged for about ten years in financing the blacksmiths (Ghantra) to prepare iron wares and then selling those themselves at distant markets to earn profits. Some of them were also at loss when some rich people of this village had mortgaged out their inferior land to these people on usufructuary terms and took possession of the land without returning the money after the expiry of seven years, or even before that, showing the example of the introduction of OLR Act, 19 of 1975. Since the oustee Kultas were late entrants into the land market of this village, naturally they bought some of the peripheral land and hence their fields also suffer from lack of irrigation because those are at the tail end of the village. Three households of Kultas were cheated of at least Rs. 3,000 by a Brahmin of a distant village with the assurance that they would get enhanced compensation on their joint property and also for the pond and tank for which they had not got any compensation. The Kulta Gountia who was used to leisurely life and never used to hard labour engaged labourers for agricultural production. He had to sell off four trucks of paddy before coming here because he did not have the place or good house to keep and had to buy paddy at a higher price later on for paying the labourers and meeting domestic consumption. His generous nature in selling things, from his shop, on credit, and the non-repayment by people led to the closure of the shop which he had opened in the initial years. He got the compensation for the *bhogra* land ten years after shifting. Five Kulta households suffered heavy loss in a litigation for seven years when the land they had purchased without registration, by prior payment, was denied by the ex-owner. It may also be noted that their marriages were delayed because of immediate economic decline and lack of accommodation in the initial years. One of them had been envied by the people of this village because as a clever man he bribed the Revenue Inspector and got two acres lease land on the government grazing land on ERRP scheme — which is usually available to the landless SCs/STs.

As in the resettlement colony, so also here, the Kultas who came from the river banks and used to rather a leisurely life and plenty of harvest of different varieties that gave them virtual self-sufficiency — they did not buy anything except kerosene, salt and clothes — had to lead a hard life and they are still doing so, repenting/remembering their prosperous past. Their internal cooperation, close proximity of their houses to each other, informal exchange of labour and livestock and their kinship linkage has however enabled them to withstand many humiliations from the natives and the tragedy of displacement. Now they are no more rootless. However, they are hardly in a position to influence the natives as it always happens in case of resource/skill-poor minority.

The four households of Gandas, who came from partly submerged villages, stayed back in the villages for two years. They did not have land of their own. They were employed round-the-year in their old villages and since attached labour was secured and remunerative in those areas, they were happy. Further, they could get firewood, fish and leafy vegetables from the Nature. When big cultivators left the village, they lost the employment opportunities and were forced to shift to this village because of relatives, of one household, and for employment opportunities in such a big village close to a semi-urban centre and also to the forest which is a good eight km. away. While shifting they were not provided with any transport; they shifted their own belongings on bullock carts because they were afraid that they might have to pay for it. It means that people were not explained or aware of the facilities provided to them. One household did not get any compensation because of strained relation between the heirs and their lack of coordination, to be available at a place on a particular date. All of them take to different sorts of labour and also manage by brick-making, selling of forest produce, dealing in goats and coarse clothes and cultivation of groundnut on ceiling surplus land. All of them are living from hand-to-mouth. In the resettlement colonies the oustees managed somehow by bidi making if nothing else was available; here that opportunity is also not available. However, the nearness to Bhatli, a small town, enables them to get different labour works round-the-year and fetches them money, equivalent to wage labour, for anything they can collect from the forest by bribing the forest officials.

Rehabilitation in the PWV

The PWV is just about half a km. from Bargarh canal, 24 km. from Bargarh and 30 km. from Sambalpur. It is presently 10 km. away from the foot-hills of Barapahar forest. Before the introduction of irrigation the villagers depended on agriculture — which was not very remunerative because of thin and infertile soil — and collection of forest produce. The village was notorious for theft so much so that wherever these people went the hosts became conscious of their presence. Overall it was a poor village with hardly five households having earthen tiles-clad houses.

Most of the oustees, who have settled here, have stayed alongside their caste members and almost at one end of the village which was earlier being used as burial ground. Hence they are easily identified. Some Saharas were earlier staying inside the village but had to shift outside because their neighbour Sahara Jhankar closed their entry — since they had to pass through his plot — and shouted at them, for many days, in drunken state. Most of the oustees knew about this village before evacuation through trade route, and contacts in weekly markets. They came here because of availability of substantial land in reasonable price, relatives and acquaintances, closeness to the forest and availability of round-the-year agricultural labour (after irrigation). Some of the oustees had gone to settle in the resettlement colonies but came back due to poor harvest, unemployment and destruction of crops by elephants. Some of them had settled in some other villages for a few years, but found it difficult to make both ends meet, and again shifted to this village. Initially, they were welcomed in this village because of relatives and requirement of extra-hands (labour force) in the wake of irrigation, land reclamation and intensive agricultural operations.

The Saharas, the Mirdhas and the Gandas were cheated most in relation to land. The land they purchased was much less than what was recorded in the registered deeds; the land they had cleared for personal cultivation was taken over forcibly by the natives when their heads of the households were unable to cultivate the land for some reason. The land they had mortgaged in on usufructuary basis was seized by the LDB because the mortgager of the land had attached those to the LDB; and the land to be purchased and already paid for was taken back by the seller because the head of the household died in the mean time. There was also discrimination in the allotment of ceiling surplus land giving last preference to them and allotting the virtually uncultivable land, and not allowing them to take possession of the allotted land. They were dissuaded from clearing grazing and fallow land available in the village; were threatened for constructing houses on plots sold to them (without registration) and were asked market price for those plots. The land orally sold to them by the Gountia has sometimes been left in the ceiling surplus land and there has also been alteration of inferior plots with the land cleared and improved by them, during consolidation. The oustees who did not have roots in the village underwent lots of trouble consequently — notwithstanding their relatives in the village.

The Kultas who came from one fully sub-merged village, spent all the compensation money in buying and reclaiming land, construction of houses and mortgaging/leasing-in land. All of them worked very hard in land reclamation. They earned wage in canal construction, transportation of timbers and boulders, agricultural labour; made earnings from the forest produce, petty trading in paddy, transportation of paddy to the ferry *ghat*, sale of leafy mattress and milk; cultivation of non-conventional cash crops like ginger and garlic and using of cowdung-cakes as fuel, etc. They are gradually coming back to their earlier positions through hard labour, miserly habits, mutual cooperation in exchanging labour and live stock, and the assured profit from irrigated agriculture. The native Kultas are necessarily envious of them because the oustees came here very helpless. The oustees have not been able to clear much fallow land because the prosperous Kultas of the village earmarked much of it alongside their agricultural land. The situation has been so precarious that there is virtually no land in this irrigated village which remains uncultivated. As a result there is no grazing land and the cattle have to be taken close to the forest for grazing. The villagers have to walk considerable distance to defecate and very often they do so on the either sides of the road and the feeder canals to avoid walking long distance. The Kultas have been able to recapture their past economic status, at least partially, in the face of all odds by proper use of the compensation and through their cultural traits — which has been true for all the localities of our study. Only one household has declined considerably in the economic ladder because it first went to San Kundesara Camp to have more land in cheaper prices and suffered repeated loss due to destruction of crops by elephants, death of the male head of the household, and small children. Now they have a dilapidated house in this village because of the non-cooperation among the brothers.

Most of the Saharas had enough land in their old village at Mudomahul and Resham, and had got proportionate compensation but most of them were instigated by the Kultas to invest their money in new ventures with which the Saharas were not used to. They also took to regular consumption of meat and liquor; loaned out money and paddy to relatives in the village which were not repaid at all. The blunder they committed was that they did not buy land immediately. Now some of them are living on agricultural labour and sale of leaves, firewood and other minor forest produce. One household, having been forced to shift his house from inside the village had to sell all the silver and part of the gold to construct a house. Later it sold the rest of the gold, it had purchased during the payment of the compensation, to buy two acres of land. Only one household of Sahara who had got substantial compensation and who bought five acres of land immediately looks like a prosperous man but physically the couple have completely worn out due to hard labour for land reclamation and earnings from different sources.

One Ganda household has also substantially improved because of substantial compensation, avoidance of liquor, buying of nine acres of agricultural land, miserly habit and his general awareness through primary education, and hard labour. But since he has a small family and no male member to support him he is leasing out some plots of land which are two km. away from the village. Rest of the Ganda oustees are agricultural labourers and the female members collect and sell forest produce because the male members are increasingly being harassed by the forest officials. All of them live from hand-to-mouth and reside in dilapidated houses.

One household of Chamar, who had 15 acres of land in the old village, first went to resettlement camp and purchased 14 acres of land there, but four of his step-brothers chased him out without giving him a share in the land. He went to his father-in-law's place, borrowed some money, and finally settled in this village. The whole family worked very hard, sold forest produce, made and repaired musical instruments, sold about 20 pairs of hand-made shoes per week and leased in 18 acres of land of the absentee Gountia very cheaply for four years and gradually came up to buy two acres of good land. However, regular habit of drinking has not helped them very much. The other Chamars are working as agricultural labourers and are poor.

The Keuts have some land of their own and they also earn some profit from making parched rice. Their condition is so so but they are not in a position to fish as they were doing in their old villages. For them, it is almost a change of occupations. One household came and constructed the house, bought land but could not pull on and left for some relative's place; again found it difficult to manage and came back here.

The Mirdha household, who had once 15 acres of land in this village, sold it gradually because of drinking habits. The Kultas of this village who bought the land from him either did not pay the amount settled, or registered more land than settled for, when he was in drunken state. Gradually, he had to borrow from the Pathan money-lender of Paharsirgida, at usurious rate of interest, which he could not repay and was slapped by him. He felt humiliated and left the village. Now his brother-in-law is looking after the property. He mortgaged most of his land to marry off his sisters-in-law and in litigation. He is now trying to reclaim the land which has been purchased by the people from a tribal without the permission of the Tahsildar; the cases are in the court and many people in the village have been involved in it.

The Dumbals, who are traditionally good cultivators, are doing very well because they had got good compensation and used the money to buy agricultural land and have good houses.

One household of Dhuba (washerman), who was quite well-off in the old village because of jajmani works in five of the nearby villages and some rent-free land given by the Gountia of the village, has suffered a lot in this village because he seemed quite well off and people did not call him for agricultural labour, and he did not have jajmani linkage with the new villagers. So he took to new ventures — selling of dehusked rice and grass from the dyke, in the nearby towns. His knowledge of pressing clothes — which the other washermen in the village did not know — has helped him gradually to recover from the economic shock. Unfortunately we did not have the occasion to encounter many of such people who traditionally lived on jajmani services.

During the period 1970-85, most of the people in this village took to petty-trading in paddy and more so in rice. They bought paddy, boiled it, dehulled it in the hullers in the village or in nearby village and sold it to people, on the other side of the river Mahanadi, who came to purchase it daily and more so on the market days — Tuesday and Saturday. The trade has declined almost to nil after 1985 because three boats upturned in the river resulting in loss of life and property, and also because of the decreasing gap of difference of price of paddy and rice on either sides of the river. People who used their carts and cattle for transportation also made good profit because they could earn Rs. 35 to Rs. 60 per trip to the ferry *ghat*. People of this side bought potato, onion, solidified *gur*, fish and axes, etc. on cheaper prices from people on the other side of the river. People of this village could earn remunerative wages from cutting bamboos for the OPM by shuttling to places on the other side of the river. This way there was some economic and social contact between people on either sides of the river. These two activities required some prior resources for investment and consumption capital, and the Pathan money-lender from Paharsirgida financed them by charging usurious rate of interest. Despite the 'availability' of formal finance from the PACS at the same place Paharsirgida and right under the nose of the police station, this usurious practice could continue because of the rigidity in formal financing and the collaboration of the forest officials, local Zamindar, the police and the Pathan money-lender. However, he has not been lending to people of this village for the last 10 years because once the villagers borrowed substantial amount and did not repay, and did not go to borrow anymore.

The absorption of substantial oustee population has been possible and has not been resented because of the big size of the peasant village having capacity for absorption in labour market of this village or of the neighbouring villages/town. The requirement of agricultural labourers in the PWV has, especially, been so much that recently 14 households of Khadias and 15 households of Mirdhas with population of 65 and 74 respectively have settled in the outskirts of the village and 60 per cent of them are oustees who had settled elsewhere but came here because of economic compulsion. This incidence proves beyond doubt that the oustees have not been properly rehabilitated as yet. However, the heavy checking in the forest, in recent times, because of scandal involving a very wealthy man of this area; the gradual increasing distance of the forest, and severe depletion of natural resources of all sorts might put the landless households in a tight situation.

Comparison

Before the influx of the oustees, the PWV was economically poorer and locationally at a much disadvantageous position compared to the PDV. After irrigation and the influx of the oustees it has become prosperous and now it is connected by canal roads. Although the PDV and the PWV are close to each other in terms of number of households and total population, the latter has much more oustees than the former. The absorption of the oustees in the labour market could be possible in the PDV because of its close location to a semi-urban commercial locality Bhatli and also because of opportunities like construction activities and forest resources. In the PWV the absorption could be possible primarily in agriculture, and trading in rice/paddy, and also to some extent in forest produce. Coincidentally both the villages did not have anybody depending on bidi making. In both the villages the oustees came from several villages and from different social groups. Although they had relatives in these villages, they are still discriminated against, and more so in the wet village. In both the villages the oustees have almost no say in the decision making bodies and they are immediately identified in terms of separate location from the main village. In both the villages Kultas have been doing well and are trying to revive their economic past, but they seem to be doing better in the PWV. They are doing better than the other caste/tribal groups because of their relentless 'greed' for land, miserly habits, hard labour, and a strong zest for survival.

(C) Rehabilitation in the Sub-urban Villages

The two sub-urban villages are at a distance of 18 km. from each other. The SDV is close to Burla town, the centre of learning in this district, which sprung up during the construction of the Hirakud dam initially housing the officers, workers and contractors related with canal and electricity deptt. Since 1963, it is under the Notified Area Committee. The SWV is 2 km. away from the South end of Sambalpur town which grew over years because of its trade, administrative and cultural network. Sambalpur was a town since 1881, whereas Burla town is of very recent origin.

Rehabilitation in the SDV

People who came to settle in the SDV, the Ganda, Rajput and Karana, were/are working with something related to Hirakud dam. When they got retrenched after the dam construction and when they had to move from their native village, they settled in this village which was very close to the dam, just 2 km. away. Rest of them came here to stay with relatives. It is an irony that although the main power channel is physically dividing the village, there is no irrigation facility in this village because of higher elevation. And water was not lifted by pump because of the vested interest of the Gountia — who wanted to get rid of the land ceiling laws to retain more land which would not have been possible if the land were irrigated. The natives of the village also lost significant amount of land (57 per cent) because land was acquired for canal construction and related activities in 1948 (see Table 6.6). It was partly like the 'dry sub-mergence' for this village. As a result the economy of the village got diversified. Renting out of houses, fishing, white/blue-collar works, shopkeeping and contract works, and non-agricultural labour became the main sources of earning for the villagers. Whereas the natives of this village lost land and thought agriculture to be rather a secondary activity — for many people the small chunk of land they retained did not seem to be an economic proposition — the oustees who settled here and who had some money bought/mortgaged in primarily double-cropped agricultural land in nearby villages and have some secured income.

The Karanas who were Gountia in their partly sub-merged old village had got Rs. 95,000 as compensation and Rs. 7,000 as *dakshina* (part of the compensation paid to Gountia) from the tenants, took to

TABLE 6.6: Distribution of Resources in the SDV

Castes/ Tribes	No. of h.h	% to the total	Total Popln.	% to the total	Amt. of land (in acres) 1902	Amt. of total land (in acres) 1948	Amt. of land (in acres) 1987	Amt. of land per h.h (in acres)	Pair of Bullocks	Amt. of land per pair of bullocks (in acres)	No. of h.h of oustees	Population of oustees
Brahmin	16	9.82	96	10.67	205	365	144	9	6	24	0	0
Rajput	2	1.23	16	1.78	0	0	0	0	2	—	2	16
Karana	3	1.84	17	1.89	0	0	0	0	0	0	3	17
Chhanapati	1	0.61	11	1.22	0	0	0	0	1	—	0	0
Goud	23	14.11	117	13.00	72	188	65	2.83	14	4.64	1	2
Keut	28	17.18	186	20.67	115	73	40	1.43	4	10	3	11
Kumbhar	6	3.68	38	4.22	49	26	19	3.17	5	3.80	0	0
Dhuba	1	0.61	4	0.44	0	0	0	0	0	0	0	0
Bhandari	2	1.23	12	1.63	0	0	0	0	2	—	0	0
Ghantra	11	6.75	65	7.22	0	0	0	0	0	0	0	0
Pap	8	4.91	37	4.11	22	25	31	3.88	4	7.75	0	0
Ganda	8	4.91	37	4.11	0	0	0	0	0	0	5	24
Ghasia	1	0.61	12	1.33	0	2	2	1	1	1	0	0
Sahara	45	27.61	209	23.22	404	260	80	0.51	23	3.48	0	0
Jhara	8	4.91	43	4.78	0	0	0	0	0	0	0	0
Total	163	100.01	900	99.99	867	939	381	2.34	62	6.15	19	93

Notes: 1. Amount of land (in acres) have been rounded up in columns 6-8 for convenience.
2. The Brahmins have also one tractor.

white-collar works after buying 3.5 acres of agricultural land in a nearby village and one of them has a small shop because he was retrenched from the job; he is also renting out portion of his house. However, their present overall status is nothing compared to the earlier one. After retirement they are planning to invest their money in business or contract work since income from land will not be enough even to maintain their present status.

Initially, for a few years after the sub-mergence, they had 12 attached labourers and 35 acres of private jungle. The head of the household kept on thinking about the bygone days. It is difficult to think that a Gountia became an ordinary man in a new village where another Gountia had considerable influence and he did not command any respect from the villagers. They cultivated 3 acres of government acquired land on lease but handed back it to the Revenue deptt. after repeated destruction by stray cattle and pigs. One of the brothers has also been a member of the NAC, giving him some prestige.

The Rajputs who had 22 acres of land in the old village and got Rs. 12,000 as compensation had combinedly purchased 6 acres of land in a village but were not given any share by the other relatives; so they came here and worked as boatmen in the dam. They had also lost 1 truck of paddy and 1 truck of timber to a relative in the other village who did not return it. Now they are landless and have constructed house on a government plot. They are living on fishing, leasing-in of land, agricultural labour, and blue-collar work in the dam, but overall their condition is so so. If one of them would not have been getting Rs. 700 per month as watchman in the dam, they would have found it difficult to pull on. Now they have kept 20 heads of cows and earn some money from the sale of milk and cowdung.

The childless Goud couple did not get any compensation since the man was working in the army, far off his village, and then opted out of it to work in the dam. After retirement he has invested the money in mortgaging in wet land in nearby villages and live on it.

The Keuts are living on fishing in the reservoir; carpentry and leasing out of little land. Two of the households have purchased double-cropped land in distant villages and living on the *kar*, i.e., the fixed amount of paddy, they get from the land. They also earn something from carpentry and non-agricultural labour. The household which is living on fishing is worse off because they spent the Rs. 5000 compensation on conspicuous consumption and did not buy any land.

They could not earn much initially because of small children.

All the Gandas are living on non-agricultural labour of different sorts. They were landless and came here primarily to work in dam and to earn something from the nearby forest which is now virtually bald and depleted.

The Saharas who came here because of relatives, expected earnings from non-agricultural labour and forest, are slightly better off than the Gandas. They are still depending on such sources alongwith some leasing in of non-irrigated land in this village and get some paddy to manage for 4 months, if the rainfall is normal and timely. Some of them have suffered a lot because of temporary shifting to other villages, dispute in compensation, expenditure in medical treatment and litigation. Only one household has 1 acre of irrigated land in a distant village which has been mortgaged out to meet medical expenditures and performing the funeral rites of the dead. It was reported by the respondents that within years after shifting, in many families, many immediate relatives have died. The expenditure on their treatment, the loss of work and earning while attending to them, the mental trauma, and the expenditure on rites after death is substantial.

Since there is no surplus land in the village for distribution in ceiling or no government grazing land to be encroached upon, and there is not much ground for clash of interests, there is not much insider-outsider feeling as regards the oustees. However, there is one ground : some of the oustees and the outsiders (white-collar workers who rent in and stay in this village to attend to their duty in Burla and Sambalpur) have more often been in a superior position because of compensation money and regular income from white-collar jobs. They lease in the acquired land allotted by the government on auction. The natives feel that their own land — which was acquired during dam construction — is not being given to them and outsiders and oustees with ready cash have been favoured. The truth is that these outsiders had cash to pay when the Revenue deptt. demanded for it; and they also took risk initially when there was lot of destruction of crops by stray cattle and pigs and when the villagers backed out.

Rehabilitation in the SWV

The SWV, situated on the earlier trade route between Jharsuguda and Sambalpur, is just 2 km. away from the South end of Sambalpur town. It has been connected by a pucca road since 1984 and is under the jurisdiction of Sambalpur NAC after 1989. This village has received maximum number of oustees amongst the six villages who contribute 22.19 per cent of the total population. The oustees are within the fold of caste/tribe category available in this village. The village has offered maximum opportunities to the oustees. Land was available, for purchase, in this village. Lot of land was available for lease-in because of the absentee Karana Zamindar family who owned 134 acres of land in 1922 and most of whom even now remain out of the village to pursue white-collar jobs (see Table 6.7). Then there is bidi making, agricultural labour, petty-trading in rice, round the year; stone-crushing, stone-digging and stone-cutting works occasionally or maximum for 6 to 8 months in a year for the last 5 years; and sale of forest produce until 1970. All these opportunities show that able-bodied people who want to work will not remain unemployed and will not starve since the wage rate is the highest (Rs. 8 per day) amongst all the localities that we have discussed. Access to formal education has been an additional advantage as realised by the oustees of late — which they would not have got easily if they would have been in their old villages.

All the Kulta households who came to resettle here had their in-laws' in this village; the relatives made their stay and search for land comfortable, economic and easier. All except one household, have still cordial relation with their in-laws' family. All the oustee Kultas had good amount of land in the old villages and they have almost been able to revive their economic past with one exception that the output in their old villages was much more; the cost of production was less, and life was much easier and happier in the old villages. Here, all of them had to toil very hard and live miserly to earn from bidi making, petty trading in rice and cultivation of own/leased-in/mortgaged-in land. A man, who is not used to hard work, has opened a shop and also makes profit from the sale of sugar, kerosene, etc. in a government ration shop. All of them also built good houses because of the easy availability of timber and cheapness of earthen tiles those days. One household that did not buy land immediately, expecting a share from his brothers staying in other villages, could not buy it anymore later because of increasing price of land. He cultivates lease-in land, earns substantially from bidi making and the sale of sweet meat. One household, which came from a partly

TABLE 6.7: Distribution of Resources in the SWV

Castes/ Tribes	No. of h.h.	% to the total	Total Popln.	% to the total	Amt. of land (in acres) 1902	Amt. of total land (in acres) 1922	Amt. of land (in acres) 1987	Amt. of land per h.h. (in acres)	Pair of Bullocks	Amt. of land per pair of bullocks (in acres)	No. of h.h. of oustees	Population of oustees
Brahmin	3	1.21	29	2.38	0	0	5	1.67	2	2.50	0	0
Karana	4	1.62	52	4.27	109	134	95	23.75	6	15.83	0	0
Oriya	9	3.64	54	4.43	38	40	41	4.56	15	2.73	0	0
Kulta	46	18.62	265	21.74	221	222	266	5.78	96	2.77	6	30
Penra	3	1.21	15	1.23	16	17	22	7.33	2	13.00	0	0
Goud	14	5.67	50	4.10	4	4	6	0.43	4	1.50	3	15
Kumbhar	4	1.62	27	2.21	0	0	0	0	1	—	0	0
Keut	8	3.24	44	3.61	14	12	11	1.38	3	3.67	0	0
Bhandari	4	1.62	20	1.64	0	0	0	0	2	—	0	0
Luhura	2	0.81	9	0.74	5	5	5	2.50	1	5.00	0	0
Pap	13	5.26	46	3.77	5	6	6	0.46	0	—	9	31
Ganda	18	7.29	74	6.07	0	7	8.50	0.72	2	4.25	9	40
Ghasia	5	2.02	34	2.79	0	0	1.50	0.30	1	1.50	0	0
Kandha	26	10.53	128	10.50	36	31	28	1.08	20	1.40	3	14
Gond	57	23.08	239	19.61	4	4	7.70	0.14	14	0.55	12	55
Sahara	25	10.12	105	8.61	0	0	0	0	8	—	16	64
Khadia	4	1.62	18	1.48	0	0	0	0	0	0	0	0
Oraon	2	0.81	10	0.82	0	0	0	0	0	0	0	0
Total	247	99.99	1219	100.00	452	482	500.70	2.03	177*	2.83	58	259

Notes: 1. * The Karanas and the Kultas have one tractor each.
2. Amount of land during 1902-87 has been rounded up for convenience.

submerged village, did not get compensation for the house until it was demolished. They are still fighting a legal case entrusting it entirely to a lawyer on the promise of one-third of the compensation money — until now they have not received compensation relating to three private ponds and a tank which are not submerged. They had also spent considerably on a piece of land bought from a Ganda in the village for which the litigation continued for seven years resulting in their win and possession of the land. The Kultas are genuinely greedy for land and would not hesitate to go for prolonged litigation even for a small parcel of land.

Among Gouds two out of the three households came here because of in-laws in the village. Before submergence they were living on agriculture and cattle rearing, i.e., selling of milk, cowdung and bullocks/cows; and tending cattle of the village. All of them were managing smoothly. One household first went to a resettlement colony, purchased there 12 acres of land out of which he ought to have got six acres but he got only three acres and for which litigation is continuing for many years. He left the colony after seven years and now cultivating one out of the three acres of land by shuttling, and leasing out the rest. That is, the household is neither here nor there. Now they are doing all sorts of labour works and three of the family members are making bidis. One household of Goud is tending the cattle of the village and is well-off even without land because of his total earnings from wage, cowdung and extra remuneration and also from *bidi* making. The other household who was doing well to begin with because of small family, earnings from *bidi* making and lease-in land, has been shattered by mishaps in the family — his eleven years-old son died, wife became mad and died — for which he had to sell 250 *tolas* of silver, three *tolas* of gold, one pair of bullocks and five heads of cow. Now the household earns livelihood from *bidi* making and all sorts of labour work.

There are three households of displaced Kandhas. All of them, came for their relatives in this village. One of them who were doing well in the old village, are doing better because three brothers took to education and later to salaried services. One son supervises the four acres of land and cultivates it with two attached labourers because he shuttles from a nearby town. The help of their relatives, who are the Jhankars of this village, has been substantial in their up-coming. The protective discrimination policy for the ST has also helped them in getting jobs; and nearness to Sambalpur helped in getting inexpensive education. The other two households had to struggle a lot and took to all sorts of labour works. Now one household earns from bidi making, parched rice selling, small shop and the regular income of a typing instructor. The other household boasts of a graduate and gifted football player who has been offered a job in State Police and they are expected to do well from a regular monthly income. It shows that education and reservation of jobs have been very helpful to the Kandhas. So all the displaced Kandhas are now in a position to find their roots again.

Among the Gonds only two households had Jhankari land; rest of them were landless in their old village and they are still so. All of them earn their livelihood from different types of labour activities and bidi making. Some of them prefer to remain attached labourers rather than work as casual labourers because of security and the availability of loan in case of the former. But they told unanimously that the condition of the attached labourers was much better in the old village. The two Jhankar households did not get compensation on their rent-free land and they spent substantially on litigation on the Jhankari rights. One of them was also cheated by his brother-in-law who took away all the compensation money kept with him and fled away to his in-law's place and stayed there. Most of the Gonds had stayed two to twelve years — usually with relatives — in other places but left those because of single crop, unemployment, etc., and came here later to have round-the-year employment. Only one household has been able to cultivate two acres of lease-in land with a pair of bullocks because four members of his family earn regularly from bidi making and also from petty-trading in rice; now the man is a *bidi munsi*. One household had to repay 80 per cent of the compensation money to a money-lender because the lender inflated the amount after the death of the male head of the household. It may be noted that all the Gonds were doing petty-trading in rice at some time or the other. Even though it was profitable it is limited because it is not a round-the-year job. The Gonds did not have the initial capital to expand their trade, and in recent time the profit has declined because firewood has been very costly (Rs. 50 per qtl.) and there is no forest nearby.

All the Pap households, except one, were landless in the old villages and do not have any land here also. Only one household has 6.5 acres of dry land in a nearby village. Since the male head is dead and the only daughter is a school teacher, the land is leased out. Only this household is managing properly; rest of the people earn their livelihood from different types of labour and bidi making. Two of the households have, recently, leased in some land after buying bullocks from their past savings. They were working as attached labourers for a long time and have recently taken to casual labour. Some of the Pap households came here because of relatives/acquaintances; others came to eke out a living. Three of the households are facing ejection out of their house-sites because the land bought by them from the Kultas had not been registered.

All the Sahara households were landless in the old village, and came here primarily to earn their livelihood by labour works after they were informed of the opportunities by their ex-Gountia who has settled in Sambalpur. They did not have relatives here but they were welcomed by the-then Zamindar to employ them as attached labourers. They have done all sorts of labour works available in the village, bidi making, and petty-trading in rice. Only for the last two years one household, which has been able to produce a police constable, has been leasing in some land for cultivation. Another Sahara, who has been working as the head attached labourer *(khamari)* of the Zamindar ever since he came here, has also alleviated his economic status by the help of the Zamindar and has got one acre of ceiling surplus land for personal cultivation. His son is now working in the Central Reserve Police and he is hoping for a bright future. He also commands respect from the villagers because of his link with the most prosperous man in this village.

Amongst the Ganda only four households had land in the old village and two of them had got more than Rs. 3,000 in compensation. All of them spent their money in eating and drinking, as admitted and reported by them. They did not buy land in this village and all of them are landless; they do not have bullocks, nor ceiling surplus land. The eleven acres of surplus land has gone to the native inhabitants of the village and none to the oustees. It was reported by them that they had appealed to the District Collector to allot the oustees a big piece of land near the village and it was considered by the Collector. However, all the notices for this purpose, which are usually pasted on the temple-walls of the village, were torn by the Kultas since they thought that land to the oustees would mean independence for them and scarcity of labourers for their agricultural operations. The Gandas are very vocal, especially against the Kultas, whom they consider the people who are stopping the flow of all the government help meant for them. They want ceiling surplus land. All of them are earning livelihood from the sources that we have mentioned for the other villagers. The displaced Gandas have constructed their houses on government grazing land. Two households who had constructed houses on grazing land in the middle of a Kulta's up-land are finding it difficult to move because the area is now being used for vegetable gardening and has to be fenced allowing no route for their movement. Now they cannot afford to buy a piece of land from the Kulta to have connection/outlet to the road. All the Ganda oustees have straw-thatched houses and many of those are in dilapidated condition.

Since 90 per cent of the oustees are living on one extreme end of the village and identified by different names, there is not much social interaction in such a big village. Hence, there is a clear feeling of insiders and outsiders even though some of the relatives of the oustees are there in the village. The death of the close relatives of the earlier times — from both sides — necessarily dilutes the relationships. Most of the oustees, except the Kultas and to some extent the Kandhas and Pap, are landless and they depend on agricultural labour, though bidi making especially for women, is also equally important. Most of the employers are from Karana, Oriya, Penra and Kulta castes. So there is a clear distinction between the employer and the employee; the natives and the oustees, and people who live in the main village and the outskirts. It is alleged by the labourers that the Kultas do not pay them the minimum wage, pay inferior paddy, manipulate the dry measures and in case of attached labourer deduct fine for absence. They also charge interest on loan advance taken out of the lump sum amount for yearly attachment (*nistar*) if borrowed in the first half of the year, and that increasingly the employers are employing migrant labourers from Madhya Pradesh during peak agricultural operations. The employers allege that the labourers of the village do never work for eight hours a day; that they are least interested in the work and use delayed tactics for casual labour. The oustees do not prefer to do things on contract because the employer always deflates the size of the plot for transplanting, weeding, and harvesting. So there is under-utilisation of labour as a result of which both the employers and the employees suffer loss.

Comparison and Conclusion

Comparing the situations in the two sub-urban villages we conclude that even though the presence of the poor oustees is welcome in the labour scarce SWV their relative physical distance from the main village and the hostile and exploitative attitude of the Kultas and other employing castes have alienated them so much so that now they are not hesitating to take to non-agricultural labour even outside the village, which they did not do earlier. More over, there is no religious/cultural activities in the village which could bind them together. On the other hand, the habitation of the oustees inside the SDV, the performance of *Nam Yajna*, and the collective respect for the Brahmin Gountia presents a more coherent picture, and the oustees have not felt that much of deprivation. Further, the employer-employee relationship is hardly found in the SDV because except the Brahmins and the Karanas nobody employs casual labourers, not to speak of attached labourers, and the oustees as others are free to take to any job they like, mostly in the non-agricultural sector.

After the discussion on rehabilitation of the oustees in the six different types of villages, it would have been interesting to compare those and discuss the hypothesis that people are most likely to settle in the SWV and least likely to settle in the TDV. We are not doing it at this stage to avoid repetition at the end. However, a comparison of the different localities of rehabilitation in terms of household, total population and the number of oustees (see Table 6.8) gives us some idea about the nature of displacement and rehabilitation. The number of households and the total population has increased in the host villages because of influx during 1951-61. The population of the oustees has increased from the TDV to PDV, SDV, TWV, PWV to SWV, and further the percentage of oustees in the wet villages are usually higher than dry villages in the corresponding categories. This indicates that an agrarian population is likely to move to a village which can offer opportunities in terms of agriculture and allied activities. Since the demand for labour and the wage rate is higher in the wet village vis-a-vis the dry village, a land-poor peasantry is more likely to move into the wet villages and hence necessarily to sub-urban wet village if congenial conditions exist. However, it should not be immediately inferred that the economic principle of rationality applies in the tribal and peasant settings as in the industrial-urban context. During the imminent hours of displacement, as in the case of death, social factors might be more crucial and prevailing than the economic ones.

TABLE 6.8: Distribution of Households, Population (1951-88) and Oustees in Different Localities

Name of the Locality	No. of Households in different years				Total Population in different years				Oustees in 1987-88			
	1951	1961	1971	1987-88	1951	1961	1971	1987-88	No. of h.h	% to the total h.h	Popln.	% to the total popln.
Kudopali	85	—	—	85	275	—	—	405	85	100%	405	100%
Kashipali	—	—	—	102	—	—	—	409	102	100%	409	100%
Pudhapara	128	76	63	85	489	294	282	410	*	*	*	*
Sapne	139	47	41	44	444	159	169	209	44	100%	209	100%
TDV	56	60	68	64	153	220	237	300	12	18.75	74	24.67
TWV	—	—	—	100	—	—	—	552	17	17.00	112	20.29
PDV	151	231	192	207	644	765	789	937	18	8.70	75	8.00
PWV	77	131	192	200	430	569	825	992	42	21.00	189	19.05
SDV	—	—	—	163	—	—	900	3	19	11.66	93	10.33
SWV	137	262	309	247	749	1058	1333	1167	58	23.48	259	22.19

Sources: 1. Census of India, District Census Hand Book, Sambalpur, Series 16, Part-B, for the years 1951, 1961 and 1971.
2. Figures for 1987-88 refer to our own enumeration during fieldwork in 1987-88.

Notes: (a) The Kashipali resettlement colony is named after the main sub-merged village Kashipali and hence the population over decades are not comparable.
(b) The population of Kudopali colony during 1961-71, is not available because it has been a part of the Sangramal Camp.
(c) Independent figures for the TWV and the SDV are not available during 1951-71.
(d) * No house got sub-merged in this village. Some of the people who left the village came back and hence cannot be treated as oustees as such.
(e) Census figures are not available for 1981.

7

CONCLUSIONS

It would not be an exaggeration to say that technology has revolutionised our life during the last three hundred years or so. This is also probably the most important factor of modernisation be it in industry, agriculture, or cultural refinement. However, it would be wrong to equate technology with human development. The central question that strikes us is whether the material gains achieved through technology has been worth the crisis, nay silent disaster, facing mankind today. We have to think seriously whether large scale deforestation, mining work, industrialisation, nuclear and military bases, construction of dams, etc. affecting the ecology, economy, and total life space of huge population, sometimes displacing them out of their native locales, can be upheld. It is not only an emotional-ethical issue but also a practical one. It goes with the assumption that such large scale, almost compulsive planned displacement is desirable; that the material gains would outweigh the overall loss (including mental trauma) to the concerned people, and the displaced people can be properly rehabilitated in such a way that they can reconstruct their past social space and develop further. Keeping this in mind we were interested in one dimension of technological development, i.e., of dam construction which is expected to be an ongoing phenomenon for quite some time. Expecting the possible scarcity of coal and the non-viability of tapping solar energy, governments in many countries have been relying on cheaper hydropower by constructing large dams. Besides generating cheaper power for electrification and industrialisation, the dams help in flood control, irrigation, navigation and supply water for human beings and industries. Most of the benefits, from such projects, however, go to urban consumers directly or indirectly. As regards the agrarian population, the people in the command area, usually leading a difficult life before the construction of the dam, gain substantially at the cost of the people in the catchment area used to leading an easy life in the fertile river basins, or tribals and 'primitive' people who depended on rivers and forests. Within the command area also the gentleman farmers, substantial owners and capitalist farmers pocket the maximum gains (Singh, 1990: 561-74). The gains and losses of such multi-purpose dam projects have been discussed at length in Chapter 1 and need no repetition. The involvement of major financial organisations like the World Bank and the IMF, in such projects, and the world-wide protest by environmentalists, several voluntary organisations and native activists have led to new thinking and alternatives to such major projects.

In India, the construction of the Hirakud dam in Orissa was one of several multipurpose river valley projects which had generated a lot of hope amongst the policy-makers and others in the post-war reconstruction period. In terms of pure and immediate economic calculation and as a measure of flood control in the economically developed and politically conscious eastern Orissa (compared to the rest of Orissa), the construction of the Hirakud dam was a historical necessity in the-then Orissa (Government of Orissa, 1968). Although there were several locational advantages regarding the site of the dam and it was completed in 'reasonable' time, the construction of the dam was a foregone conclusion and the construction work started before the feasibility report was finalised (Agarwal, 1967: 40-42; Government of India, 1947: 17). Further, the Public Accounts Committees were not satisfied with the financial handling of the project. From technical point of view there have been questions regarding cracks in the dam due to improper curing of concrete at the time of construction; and high rate of silting affecting irrigation, generation of electricity and desertification of Cuttack city. Further, the unabated release of effluents from the Orissa Paper Mills at Brajrajnagar and the industrial, domestic and municipal sewerage on to the river and the reservoir has resulted in water borne diseases and increased alkalinity of water (S. C., 1987). The reduction in the storage capacity of the reservoir from 8105 cubic km. of water in 1956 to 6427 cubic km. in 1988 has been a matter of grave concern for the planners and the people who have now been heavily dependent on the dam. On top of it the increase in the frequency of flood from 11.8 years in 1956 to 3.75 years in 1988 has belied all hopes of flood control. Despite the several benefits proclaimed by the Government the dam seems to have failed in its avowed objectives (S.C., 1988; Baboo, 1991 d).

The social dimensions of the Hirakud dam project were enormous. The declaration of the proposed construction of the dam was initially greeted with disbelief on the part of most people followed by anger and shock, on receiving notification about the acquisition of land and permanent structures in the catchment area, and on hearing about and seeing for themselves the gigantic construction that was to be undertaken. The project would mean economic disaster for a large section of them. Their protests and peaceful demonstrations were quelled by the ruling Congress both by force and by persuasion of 'sufficient' compensation, i.e., land for land and house for house (Nanda and Tripathy, 1987). The government also promised the displaced people model colonies with modern facilities and economic rehabilitation in the forest-cleared colonies. However, due to several anticipated and actual difficulties people did not wish to go and live in these camps/colonies. The government was also not in a position to provide land and shelter to the people and it panicked as the date for filling of the reservoir drew near. The government, unable to deal with the situation gave them the option to stay back in partly submerged villages or to move to old established villages. By doing so the government was able to get away with paying some minimal compensation to the affected people thus doing away with its tall promises and social responsibilities (Supakar, 1988). To date, only 10.86 per cent of the affected people have been rehabilitated in 9.61 per cent of the total area.

To comprehend a total first-hand picture about the affected population, we conducted intensive field work in ten localities of Sambalpur district, Orissa, where the displaced persons have been living in different settings. The details regarding the selection of the localities and the techniques of data collection have been spelt out in Chapter-III. We were basically interested to know about people's rationale for the selection of their future habitat, their reaction to the construction of the dam, the way they spent the compensation, their survival strategies, their social interaction in the alien environment, their opinion regarding the different rehabilitational measures of the government, and their method of reconstructing their past social space, etc.

As regards the selection of the locality, it was gathered that people usually wanted to go en block to a particular locality if cultivable land was available at least in accordance with the old village. In a few villages, the villagers did not want to go along with a particular caste group only if the latter was crooked and exploitative in nature or if they were a divided lot. The other important factors for rehabilitation were : availability of forest resources for fuel, timber and even for selling those in dog days; suitable location befitting one's vocation/occupation and the hope of having easy access to urban labour/commodity market; water and pasture for animals; protection from elephants which destroyed the crops despite strict vigilance, and some prior acquaintance with their would-be-cohabitants.

Usually poor people came to settle in the rehabilitation colonies set up by the government because the price of the land in the forest-cleared area was within their reach and they entirely depended on the government for basic amenities. They could not go to settle in old established villages where the cost of land was appreciating fast for speculative and actual demands and where the vested interests in these villages dissuaded the outsiders from buying land and settling. Whenever people went outside the government colonies and settled in old established villages they also wanted to settle in some known villages where they had some relatives/kinsmen or acquaintances but necessarily thought in terms of future sustenance. Poor people in the partly sub-merged villages chose to settle in the periphery of the reservoir or at a little distance depending on the unsubmerged land, forest and fishing. Using the economic principles of rationality one can say that the people must have chosen to mostly settle in the sub-urban wet village and least in the tribal dry village but it is not substantiated by data. In our study we see that the influx of oustees into these different villages in terms of household and population has been of this order : TDV (12:74), TWV (17:112), PDV (18:75), PWV (42:189), SDV (19:93), and SWV (58:259). It shows that the wet villages have received more oustees than the dry villages. It was observed that the oustees have not been rehabilitated properly, as yet, and are still in the process of shifting from one locality to the other. In villages where there was demand for labour the oustees have been welcomed in the initial phase but gradually in all the villages, and more so in wet villages, there has developed the feeling of 'outsiders' when the oustees, because of their hard work and the initial help from their relatives, have prospered economically. Sometimes such prosperity has been the cause of strained relationship even among relatives. Since the influx of the oustees lessened one's share in the collective resources like water, pasture and forest produce the locals resented the oustees. Even when the oustees have prospered they are not in a position to be influential politically. When the oustees went to settle in heterogenous colonies, their heterogeneous composition has not enabled them to move in along a pre-defined goal and the leadership has been very fluctuating to achieve any useful end. On the other hand, people in the homogeneous resettlement colony have been in a position to present a collective image despite differential economic interest and glaring disparity in ownership of resources. The social structure has been reproduced in such localities. The poor in the partly sub-merged villages stayed back because they depended on the cultivation of the left-over upland and sub-mergible land, fishing, and cattle rearing near the reservoir. Since the substantial land holders left the village new leadership emerged in these villages without having a commonly accepted leader. Because of uncertainty in harvest due to sub-mergence and scarcity of water (*budi* and *pudi*) these people heavily depend on non-agricultural income but the erstwhile attached labourers and casual labourers have become free to sell their labour according to their will as they also cultivate some fore-shore and land-lease land.

Many of the oustees have had to change their occupations and sometimes took to works which are usually proscribed by their caste groups. But for certain activities like petty-trading in rice, *bidi* making and collection of forest produce most of them would have found it difficult to survive. However, because of specific cultural traits the Kultas (cultivator by occupation) in all the localities have been in a position to purchase almost comparable amount of land as in the old village, and have been able to revive their past economic status. On the other hand, the SCs and STs have not been in a position to do so primarily because of their initial poor resources, and unimaginative spending on items other than land. All the respondents criticised the under-payment policy of the government and callous attitude in rehabilitation. But all of them have become too dependent on the government and have not shown much interest in collective economic upliftment.

In the initial years of resettlement the oustees in all the localities suffered a lot of hardships but there was some variation according to the locality, the resources position of the oustees and the interactional pattern of the oustees and the hosts, especially in the old established villages. People underwent maximum hardships in the resettlement colonies because they were completely uprooted and came to live in an alien set-up even though they were provided with some skeletal shelter and almost uncultivable land. People in the homogeneous colony could mitigate their hardships because they lived along with their kinfolk. People in the heterogeneous colony suffered from this respect but they had more economic opportunities because of the suitable location (This should not be generalised for all the heterogeneous colonies). Those people who moved to villages of different spatio-cultural categories suffered too. They had to arrange for the land and shelter on their own, but the hosts helped them in some cases. However, in some other cases they had to undergo lot of difficulties for the basic things in life and more so in the arena of social interaction. Oustees who had to reside in a new locality very close to their old ones suffered to some extent because the substantial holders of the land left the village due to submergence and on whom they depended for leasing in and labour. But they could manage because they cultivated the left over uplands and lease land, and also earned from non-agricultural works, fishing and cattle rearing. It seems that the people in the partly sub-merged village near the semi-urban commercial centres suffered least because they had multiple sources of earnings even though they were affected by the uncertainty of the reservoir level. Even though we have discussed different types of localities the scale of sufferings should not be generalised *ipso-facto* at a broader level even for all the oustees of the Hirakud dam, let alone other dams which have affected mostly tribals in India. This is not to say that the result of this study is just contextual specific. We are simply, stating a warning against extrapolation and suggesting that indepth studies must be conducted before such large-scale rehabilitation is attempted and that such schemes should be implemented in full consultation with the affected people.

The oustees in all the localities unanimously stated that they were not properly compensated for their agricultural land, houses and trees. They complained of irregularities, discrimination, bureaucratic hurdles, legal complications and lack of rational criteria in the payment of compensation. They were not in a position to have the same kind of assets in the new locality, with the compensation. Most of the people were not in a position to utilise or could not utilise the compensation in productive ways. Compensation in cash, and that too to people who had never seen 'so much of amount' with them, led to a lot of misuse, and more so by the poor, unlettered, lower castes and tribals. People were cheated, looted and they spent sometimes on conspicuous consumption and also on litigation, medication, pilgrimage and so on. Very few people could utilise it for productive purposes.

Overall there was a general economic decline; the 'haves', the clever and the educated took advantage of the crisis. Only the rich, educated people or the Brahmins and the artisans castes went to live in the towns because they had the skill, resources and the entrepreneurial quality to survive and prosper in the towns and also because they would not have been able to struggle in the hinterlands with little opportunities. The oustees underwent tremendous psychological set-back and they had to work very hard for survival and economic rehabilitation so much so that many of the sufferers did not survive long. This is evident from virtual absence of very old people amongst the oustees. According to them the government did not fulfill its promises in terms of the rehabilitational measures. They were also unhappy because due to their sacrifice people in the command area prospered and they had to be dependent on them later. Further, they were stigmatised as *budi anchalar loka* (reservoir oustees) for ever. The rehabilitation plan was completely unsatisfactory to most of the people because the planners and policy makers had very little interaction with the affected people and they seemed to have little knowledge about rural life. On the other hand, major decisions were imposed on the people and they were never taken to confidence, nor were they involved in the process of displacement and rehabilitation.

Because of the dislocation of such a scale and complexity the community life of the villagers got completely shattered so much so that even though only about 11 per cent of the oustees have been rehabilitated physically they are still thinking of their good old days and would not hesitate to go back to the old villages if the Hirakud dam ever burst and their native place became accessible. Overall, it can be safely stated that the oustees have not been in a position to reconstruct their past social space. Notwithstanding the political overtones behind the construction of the Hirakud dam, it may be stated that the government had good intentions : that it wanted to solve the problems of floods and droughts and wanted to encourage development in Orissa. However, the social cost was least attended to. Moreover, the government of that time, which just had got rid of the colonial clutches, could not think in terms of the distorted development it would usher in.

Today when we have heard the story of the Hirakud dam from several sources we come to the conclusion that such processes need not be repeated elsewhere in the country whereby thousands of people would be displaced from their native locales and would be compelled to sail off in to an unknown sea. The government claims that it can rehabilitate the oustees for a much better way of life; but it forgets that for an agrarian population readily cultivable land in suitable quantity as well as other related sources of livelihood are bare essentials, and that the peasants are emotionally highly attached to ancestral land and certain specific cultural performances. In recent times governments., at least in the developing countries, adopting a capitalist path of development, as in India, do prefer such giant multi-purpose projects not because of any genuine desire to develop the lot of the bulk of the down-trodden but to serve the interest of the capitalist class which helps them in coming back to power again and again. Even though we have not worked out a detailed cost-benefit analysis of the Hirakud dam we can safely infer from several research/newspaper reports that the dam has failed in its major objectives like electricity, irrigation, flood control and enhanced agricultural production. Further, the decreasing facilities from this dam would make the dependent population increasingly restless, unsure and frustrated about their future course of action (Baboo, 1991(d), 2373-79).

Studies in India and elsewhere have already suggested that small dams involving local labour, limited resources and built across small rivers and rivulets, which do not displace people or displace very few people are more useful, manageable and much less harmful in case of accidents. This will not disturb the ecology. Further, research should be carried on regarding harnessing of electricity from such small dams and also from sources other than coal and water. The mad rush for multi-purpose dams like the Hirakud dam must be stopped at the earliest. The forces of Nature must be curbed as little as possible so that man becomes its friend and not its foe.

APPENDICES

APPENDIX-I

Bench Mark and Statement showing Villages which will be Sub-merged in Hirakud Reservoir up to RL-632

Name of the Village	Affected Status (P/F)	Area (in acres)
Jharsuguda Police Station		
Gandghora	P	50.87
Remja	P	124.26
Telenpali	P	196.22
Katarbaga	P	602.37
Bundia	P	387.87
Ainlapali	P	48.97
Balput	P	452.51
Jurabaga	P	49.11
Darlipali	P	13.45
Kirarama	P	411.48
Gurhipali	P	44.57
Dudolsingha	P	925.12
Jamera	P	159.70
Jamuapali	P	85.72
Singhabaga	P	673.21
Hirma	P	227.36
Khait	P	168.20
Rampur	P	507.27
Bhursund	P	632.32
Dumermunda	P	243.40
Patrapali	P	610.04
Malda	P	236.43
Kheroal	P	110.11
Bhagipali	P	43.84
Sirpura	P	120.04
Katapali	P	11.92
TOTAL – 26	P only	

Name of the Village	Affected Status (P/F)	Area (in acres)
Sason Police Station		
Tihura	P	603.99
Balbaspur	P	68.09
Gourpali	P	313.99
Kilasama	P	1220.15
TOTAL – 4	P only	
Katarbaga Police Station		
Thelkoloi	P	104.71
Tumbekela	P	81.13
Tarekela	P	61.49
Dantamura	P	459.12
Kumbhari	P	102.38
Khinda	P	1796.77
Talabira	P	34.02
Bansimal	P	320.50
Lapanga	P	808.21
Bamaloi	P	88.23
Gurupali	P	165.93
Purhapara	P	541.90
Pandloi	P	265.08
Nisanbhanga	P	95.16
Babuchakli	P	373.01
Baunsen	P	405.71
Thuntikatarbaga	F	641.04
Sapne	F	919.22
Jogipali	F	
Kurla	F	1250.03

(*Contd.*)

APPENDIX-I (*Contd.*)

Name of the Village	Affected Status (P/F)	Area (in acres)
Salad	P	1800.78
Kudopali	F	275.17
Rengali	P	27.17
Pitapali	P	919.23
TOTAL – 24	(5F + 19P)	
Sambalpur Sadar		
Gondpali	F	220.49
Jamadarpali	P	227.53
Solbandh	P	88.21
Solpali	P	520.86
Amdi	F	420.60
Padhanpali	F	302.85
Mundapali	F	664.71
Parta	F	969.57
Bhulka	F	585.87
Saplahara	F	2470.79
Bartang	F	906.10
Junani	F	1721.76
Santang	F	513.94
Amghora	F	729.63
Chilantikud	F	151.10
Hirakud	F	829.72
Jamra	F	108.45
TOTAL – 18	(4P + 14F)	
Attabira Police Station		
Dumerpali	F	2361.83
Batimunda	F	1022.00
Nunemahulpali	F	1807.53
Burpali	F	1717.88
Dhodrokusum	P	146.54
Lohara R.F.	P	
Mundomahul	F	1166.57
Resam	F	1435.61
Barkhandia	F	6.46
Sahajbahal	F	1638.54
Chakramal	F	326.18
Pandrimal	F	574.29
Ramedega	F	574.70
TOTAL – 13	(1P + 12F)	
Ambabhona Police Station		
Tahab	F	413.14
Kurumkhel	P	1994.11
Bhulti	F	1773.83
Khairpali	F	276.76
Amlipali	F	596.93
Rengalipali	P	449.74
Govindpur	P	977.05
Bhainatora	P	15.96
Kandaipali	P	43.98
Baigapali	P	31.84
Ramkhol	P	135.76
Uttam	P	65.18
Tamdei	P	850.97
Jarimuli	P	815.24
Launsara	P	849.56
Arjunda	P	320.49
Dungri	P	106.20
Holsari	P	375.10
Sauntamal	P	15.93
Badmal	P	394.47
Behera	P	199.82
Banjipali	P	79.70
Kusumunda	P	388.56
Bugbugi	P	290.60
Antrari	P	602.01
Budhiapali	P	137.25
Chikhli	P	494.73
Ganthiapali	P	99.68
Barangakot	P	179.15
Beniapali	P	143.46
Lether	P	21.38
Ruchida	P	17.11
Bungapali	P	77.28
Ghungrapali	P	97.78
Saraipali	P	11.43
TOTAL – 34	(23P + 11F)	
Mahadevpali Police Station		
Sukhasodha	P	402.16
Semlia	P	512.88
Kandekela	P	562.72

(*Contd.*)

APPENDIX-I (*Contd.*)

Name of the Village	Affected Status (P/F)	Area (in acres)	Name of the Village	Affected Status (P/F)	Area (in acres)
Chicholi	F	314.62	*Mura Police Station*		
Mohadi	P	762.06			
Sardha	P	523.88	Baghra	F	3161.70
Chikhli	P	817.61	Dungipali	F	1378.41
Remta	P	87.36	Palsapali	F	308.71
Sodha	F		Khurigaon	F	765.96
Panchpudugia	F	24.10	Kalni	F	1895.11
Dholunda	P	432.75	Meriapara	F	1050.55
Tilgi	P	1530.04	Rampaluga	F	1868.05
Gudum	P	347.18	Ghenachal	F	708.19
Pithinda	P	680.99	Mura	F	1360.20
Nandopali	P	358.32	Jalhari	F	461.44
Amapali	P	403.57	Pandri	P	1201.16
Kanaktura	P	175.10	Urda	F	1866.21
Lubahaga	P	666.39	Benkmura	P	266.60
Bardarha	P	639.44	Patrapali	F	1279.03
Kusmulha	P	1983.37	Kutripali	P	1771.08
Ghunghutpali	P	611.74	Sunari	P	931.12
Kandijharan	P	196.60	Barhiapali	P	1072.70
Mahasingha	P	12.02	Beheramal	P	258.68
Kadamghat	P	57.01	Baghmunda	P	669.13
Baonsenpali	P	159.36	Singharpur	P.	231.41
Bhikampali	P	192.36	Dumerpali	F	838.71
Chhuhipali	P	662.43	Pandapali	F	270.20
Jampali	P	218.98	Haldi	F	307.24
Mahadevpali	F		Malda	F	805.89
Barhampur	F	63.41	Thebra	P	592.67
Padampur	P	1228.86	Sagarpali	P	1046.04
Uchpinda	F	385.24	Deoli	F	302.48
Mohanpura	F	335.71	Parsian	P	225.53
Kadamdihi	F	90.43	Bhaunrachaka	P	207.54
Andhiari	F	420.06	Sambarbaga	P	99.13
Jharupara	P	259.58	Diwanmura	P	494.76
Nachanmura	P	199.32	Kudabaga	P	1089.69
Parsada	P	873.47	Saraipali	F	736.48
Panchpudugia	F		Khajurdihi	F	576.45
Thakurpali	F	149.48	Lachipali	P	510.76
Nuapara	F	369.56	Sahasbaga	P	475.27
Pidapali	F	724.34	Ankoli	F	257.46
Jogni	F	701.09	Katarbaga	P	96.35
Kotgarh	F	1285.79	Jamgaon	P	566.79
Badimal	P	5.90	Telan	P	25.04
Charupali	P	2.92	Kuremal	P	89.04
Chikhlapali	P	7.33	Dhamdihi	F	453.86
TOTAL – 46	(28P + 18F)		TOTAL – 46 (19P + 27F)		

(*Contd.*)

APPENDIX-I (*Contd.*)

Name of the Village	Affected Status (P/F)	Area (in acres)
Rampella Police Station		
Antardol	F	1408.16
Balanda	F	3655.03
Nimuhipali	F	349.51
Kulsar	F	1038.37
Petupali	F	988.73
Darlipali	F	901.88
Burda	F	331.00
Desar	F	1470.28
Taldihi	F	958.18
Tarda	F	579.80
Kashipali	F	1680.28
Lakhanpur	F	839.11
Mangalpur	F	1004.52
Jogni	F	1658.54
Marang	F	395.71
Bhejikud	P	754.02
Piplikhani	P	595.26
Sartang	F	577.72
Botlanga	F	1100.66
Kumbharbandh	P	71.60
Rampella	P	4567.20
Tahud	F	1915.70
Gaurpali	F	379.86
Ramela	P	2497.12
Tilia	P	213.40
Singhipali	P	217.11
Barangamal	P	1238.54
Bhatli	P	1699.55
Arhapara	P	3811.65
Telenpali	P	177.50
Banharpali	P	42.65
Bhutia	P	165.45
Remra	P	683.39
Binua	P	874.02
Ghararama	F	582.29
Budla	F	742.27
Negipali	P	51.97
TOTAL – 38	(17P + 21F)	
Pusar Police Station (MADHYA PRADESH)		
Ektal	P	42.41

Name of the Village	Affected Status (P/F)	Area (in acres)
Dhanuadera	P	17.91
Netnagar	P	47.58
Badmal	P	67.44
Thengapali	P	8.06
Chhapora	P	61.18
Rengalpali	P	298.91
Kandagarh	P	306.64
Khaimuhan	P	85.36
Chhotehaldi	P	56.08
Kondpali	P	9.70
Tribhona	P	93.09
Padigaon	P	388.10
Sutupali	P	17.78
Tinnuini	P	58.65
Borajharia	P	74.05
Surajgarh	P	50.90
Nawapali	P	34.38
Total – 18	P only	
Saria Police Station (MADHYA PRADESH)		
Rebo	P	725.34
Bharatpur	P	141.55
Mohadi	P	334.72
Tora	P	344.48
Thengaguri	P	150.00
Lukapara	P	232.17
Randhidih	P	31.98
Sursi	P	54.42
Lipti	P	9.51
Sankra	P	103.17
Borida	P	399.90
Chhote-Nawapara	P	0.81
Surajgarh	P	15.82
Bijaypur	P	1.02
Chandargarh	P	16.00
Parasrampur	P	2.90
Jaipur	P	18.06
Porath	P	15.76
TOTAL – 18 (15P + 3F)		

APPENDIX-II

No. of Villages Sub-merged in the Hirakud Reservoir : A Comparison

Police Station	Fully	Partly	Total*	Fully	Partly	Total**
Rampella	24	14	38	17	21	38
Mura	27	18	45	27	19	46
Mahadevpali	18	28	46	18	28	46
Attabira	12	0	12	12	1	13
Ambabhona	12	23	35	11	23	34
Sambalpur Sadar	17	1	18	14	4	18
Katarbaga	4	20	24	5	19	24
Jharsuguda	1	25	26	0	26	26
Sason	0	3	3	0	4	4
Total (for Sambalpur Dist.)	115	132	247	108	141	249
Pusar	N.A.	N.A.	N.A.	0	18	18
Saria	N.A.	N.A.	N.A.	3	15	18
Grand Total				111	174	285

Sources: * Government of Orissa, *District Statistical Hand Book, Sambalpur*, 1966. p. 407.

** Hydrology Sub-division, Hirakud Dam Circle Office, Burla, 22.11.1986.

Note: Out of the 11 Police Stations Pusar and Saria belong to M.P. and the rest belong to Sambalpur District in Orissa.

GLOSSARY

Local words used in this work have not been arranged alphabetically. Those have been arranged under different heads according to their similarities.

Castes:
Brahmin, Gosein, Rajput, Karana, Kulta, Penra, Oriya, Kansari, Chhanapati, Mali, Goud, Teli, Sundhi, Keut, Majhian, Kumbhar, Bhat, Dumbal, Bhulia, Sial, Luhura, Ghantra, Dhuba, Bhandari, Satnami, Pap, Ganda, Dom, Ghasia, Chamar.

Tribes:
Sahara, Gond, Kandha, Binjhal, Munda, Mirdha, Bhuyan, Khadia, Oraon.

Festivals and Functions:
Ratha Yatra, Nabanna, Samalai Puja, Pousa Purnima, Dhanu Yatra, Nam Yajna, Khar Pujei, Bhagabat temple, *dakshina* (donation to a priest).

Location:
Pahilpar (on the other side of river Mahanadi), *Surua gan* (settled village), *budi anchalar loka* (reservoir oustees), Upar para (upper ward), Tali para (lower ward), *para* (ward), *basti* (settlement), *goth* (a place near the village where the herdsboys assemble the cattle), *Kachcha* road (village roads usually motorable only during the fair weather), ferry *ghat* (a location across the river frequented by the boatman), *nalia* (rivulet).

Land: *bahal* (bottom land), *benna* (del), *mal* (upland), *aat* (usually fallow or inferior upland), *khari* land (fertile land receiving organic manures especially during rainy season), *budi* (submerged), *pudi* (scarcity of water), *bhogra*, *Brahmottar mafi* (rent-free land enjoyed by the Gountias and Zamindars during

British days), *naukari mafi* (rent-free land enjoyed by the service castes/tribes), *gochar* (grazing land), *patta* (lease deed), *mutkel* (a type of soil mixed with pebbles and slates and hence unsuitable for agriculture), *fal bhogi patta* (deed conferring the right to enjoy fruits from trees on a patch of land),*kar*(a tenurial arrangement for fixed amount of rent in kinds).

Labour:

An yearly attached labourer is called a *guti*whose monthly remuneration (usually in kinds) is called *bhuti* and the lumpsum amount for the yearly attachment is called *nistar*, and the piece of land given for self cultivation is known as *bunati*. *Khamari* means head-attached labourer who usually supervises more than he works. *Hemali*is a labourer who usually lifts the load on his back. *Nariha*means water carrier usually of the Goud caste.*Munsi* is a supervisory staff helping in accounts and other matters.

Mate usually refers to someone working in canal and railway gates.

Weights and Measures: *Tola* is equivalent to 10 gms, used in the context of gold and silver.

Plants and Trees: *Kachher*, *mamer*, *kadmod*, *sunsunia* are leaves usually eaten by poor people. Flowers like *mahua* have multiple uses both for men and animals. *Amla*, *kendu*, *bel*, *char*, *tol*, etc. are usually jungle fruits and eaten in bulk only during scarcity. Similarly, roots like *kasur* and *dhulu* and shoots of bamboo, i.e., *kaddi* are consumed rarely and more so by poor people. *Daro* is used in constructing temporary shed/house and means the strait branches of young plants or trees. *Binnhi* and *Panasi* (wild grasses) and *thelko* (a jungle fruit) symbolise higher fertility of the soil. *Subabul* is a plant used as fodder. *Benacher* is a root used in chics.

Miscellaneous: *Sika* is a rope work made of jute and used to keep food items hanging away from the reach of cat, dog and reptiles. *Talei* is a mattress made of bamboo and used to dry paddy and cereals. *Dhenki* is a wooden implement used to dehusk paddy. *Dhoti* means a loin cloth usually used by males. *Gur* is unrefined sugar. *Panch rasi* is a mixed product used in a derogatory sense. *Bhang* is the powder used in making *bidi*. *Jhankar* is a tribal priest or village watchman who enjoyed rent-free land, in lieu of his service, during British days.

BIBLIOGRAPHY

Agrawal, G.D., 1967. *The Story of the Hirakud Project*. Delhi : Ministry of Irrigation and Power, Government of India.

Alvares, Claude and R. Billorey, 1988. *Damming the Narmada : India's Greatest Planned Environmental Disaster*. Dehra Dun : Natraj.

Areeparampil, Mathew, n.d. *The Impact of Subarnarekha Multi-purpose Project on the Indigenous People of Singhbhum*. Chaibasha : Tribal Research and Training Centre.

Baboo, Balgovind, 1987. "Understanding Economic Exchanges in Rural India : Towards a Framework", *Sociological Bulletin*, Vol. 36, No. 1, pp. 21-53.

Baboo, Balgovind, 1988. "Impact of Mechanisation on Rural Women : A Case of Rice-Husking Industry", in T.M. Dak (ed), *Women and Work in Indian Society*. Delhi : Discovery Publishing House, pp. 251-64.

Baboo, Balgovind, 1991(a). "Big Dams and the Tribals : The Case of the Hirakud Dam Oustees in Orissa", *Social Action*, Vol. 41, No. 3, pp. 288-303.

Baboo, Balgovind, 1991(b). "Development and Rehabilitation : A Comparative Study of Dam Oustees in Two Tribal Villages of Orissa", *Sociologus*, Vol. 41, No. 1, pp. 16-30.

Baboo, Balgovind, 1991(c). "Rehabilitation of Dam Oustees : A Comparative Study of Partly vs. Fully Sub-merged Villages in Orissa". *Indian Journal of Social Science*, Vol. 4, No. 2, pp. 287-306.

Baboo, Balgovind, 1991(d). "State Policies and People's Response : Lessons from the Hirakud Dam in Orissa", *Economic and Political Weekly*, Vol. XXVI, No. 41, pp. 2373-79.

Baboo, Balgovind, 1992. "Development and Displacement : A Comparative Study of Rehabilitation of Dam Oustees in two Sub-urban Villages of Orissa", *Man in India*, Vol. 72, No. 1, pp. 1-14.

Bandyopadhyay, J., etc., 1987. *India's Environment : Crises and Responses*. Dehra Dun : Natraj.

Behura, N.K., 1989. "Socio-Economic Problems and Social Change among the Relocatees of Rengali Dam — A Case Study", *Man and Life*, Vol. 15, Nos.1&2, pp. 1-22.

Benjamin, Rahul, 1981. *Government Delays Commission, Denies Justice* (A Case Study of the Gujarat Government's Inquiry into Commission set up to probe the Morvi Disaster). Ahmedabad : Consumer Education and Research Centre.

Centre for Science and Environment, 1982. *The State of India's Environment : The First Citizen's Report*. Delhi.

Centre for Science and Environment, 1985. *The State of India's Environment : The Second Citizen's Report*. Delhi.

Cernea, Michael, M., 1985. "Sociological Knowledge for Development Projects", in M.M.. Cernea (ed), *Putting People First : Sociological Variables in Rural Development*. New York : OUP.

Chakaraborthy, Manab, 1987. Settlement of Large Dam Oustees in India : paper presented at the *Regional Workshop on People and Dams*. New Delhi : PRIA.

Chamber, Robert, (ed), 1970. *The Volta Resettlement Experience*. London : Pall Mall.

Chandrasekhariah, K., 1965. *Rehabilitation and Social Readjustment in the Tungabhadra Water-Spread Area*. Delhi : Planning Commission.

D'Monte, Darryl, 1984. "A Question of Survival" *The Illustrated Weekly*, May 20, pp. 6-17.

Das, S.P. and S.S. Singh, 1985. "Koel Karo Hydro-Electric Project, Bihar", Working Paper, *Seminar on Big Dams in India*. Ranchi : Xavier Institute of Social Service. Feb. 18-20.

Dasgupta, Saibal, 1986. "Orissa reconsidering land for land policy" *Indian Express*, Oct.

Dhawan, B.D., 1989. "Major and Minor Irrigation Works : Cost Aspects of the Controversy", *EPW*, Vol. XXIV, No. 39, pp. A-117-21.

Dhawan, B.D., 1989. "Mounting Antagonism to Big Dams", *EPW*, Vol. XXIV, No. 20, pp. 1096-1099.

Dogra, Bharat, 1982. "Problems of Resettlement of Dam Evictees in western Himalayas", paper presented at the *Seminar on Political Economy of Rehabilitation*. Surat : Centre for Social Studies.

Dogra, Bharat, 1986. "The Indian Experience with Large Dams", in E. Goldsmith and N. Hildyard (eds), *The Social and Environmental Effects of Large Dams"*, Vol. III. *Case Studies*. Camelsford : Wadebridge Ecological Centre.

Dutta, Manju, 1977. Jamshedpur : *The Growth of the City and its Regions*. Calcutta : The Asiatic Society.

Eckholm, Erik P., 1976. *Losing Ground : Environmental Stress and World Food Prospects*. New York : Norton.

Engineer, Rusi, 1982. "To Dam or not to Dam", *Business India*, Feb. 15-28, pp. 73-75.

Fernandes, W. and E.G. Thukral (eds), 1988. *Development, Displacement and Rehabilitation*. Delhi : Indian Social Institute.

Fernandes, W., G. Menon and K.T. Chandy, 1988. *Forest Environment and Tribal Economy : Deforestation, Impoverishment and Marginalisation in Orissa*. Delhi : Indian Social Institute.

Finsterbusch, Kurt, 1980. *Understanding Social Impacts : Assessing the Effects of Public Projects*. Beverly Hills : Sage.

GASS, 1987. *A Report on Baliapal*. Balasore : Ganatantrik Adhikar Suraksha Sangathan.

Goldsmith, Edward and N. Hildyard, 1984. *The Social and Environmental Effects of Large Dams*, Vol. I, Overview. Camelsford: Wadebridge Ecological Centre.

Goodland, R., 1985. "Environmental Aspects of Hydro-Electric Power and Water Storage Projects (With Special Reference to India)", paper presented to *International Seminar on Environmental Impact Assessment of Water Resources Projects,* Dec. 12-14. University of Roorkee : Water Resources Development Training Centre.

Government of India, 1947. *Hirakud Dam Project, Mahanadi Valley Development.* Simla : Government Press.

Government of India, 1952. *Report of the Advisory Committee on Hirakud Project.* Simla : Central Water and Power Commission.

Government of India, 1953. Public Accounts Committee, 1952-53. *Sixth Report, Hirakud Dam Project.*

Government of India, 1961. Ministry of Information and Broadcasting, *Our River Valley Projects.* Delhi.

Government of India, 1979. *Register of Large Dams in India.* Delhi: Central Board of Irrigation and Power.

Government of India, 1987. *Large Dams in India.* Vol. I. New Delhi : Central Board of Irrigation and Power.

Government of India, Min. of Home Afrs., 1985. *A Report of the Committee on Displaced Tribals due to Developmental Projects.* Delhi.

Government of Orissa, 1957. Political and Services (RVD) Deptt., *Report on the Evacuation of the Sub-mergible Area of the Hirakud Dam Project for the year 1956.* Cuttack: Government Press.

Government of Orissa, 1958. *Floods in Orissa Rivers during 1955-56, Final Report,* Bhubaneshwar : Revenue (Spl). Relief Deptt.

Government of Orissa, 1968. *Report on the Benefits of Hirakud Irrigation : A Socio-economic Study.* Cuttack : Bureau of Economics and Statistics

Government of Orissa, 1980. Orissa Legislative Assembly, *36th Report.* "On Breach of Bargarh Canal"

Government of Orissa, Bureau of Economics and Statistics, 1977. *Economic Survey of Orissa,* Bhubaneshwar, pp. 195-200.

Government of Orissa, Finance Deptt., 1957. *Report of the Public Accounts Committee,* (Vol. I, pp. 12-13; Vol. II, pp. 18-21; Vol. III, pp. 110-11.)

Government of Orissa, Finance Deptt., 1958. *Report of the Public Accounts Committee* (Vol. II, pp. 64-70).

Government of Orissa, Legislative Assembly, 1959. *Report of the Public Accounts Committee* (Vol. I, p.18; Vol. II, p.8, 52-53.)

Gupta, S.P., 1989. *Planning and Development in India.* Delhi : Allied.

Hanson, Arthur J., 1981. "Transmigration and Marginal Land Development", in G.E. Manson (ed), *Agricultural and Rural Development in Indonesia.* Colorado : Westview.

Hanumantha Rao, T. and B. Bownder, 1984. *Sedimentation in Reservoir Management Issues,* Hyderabad : Administrative Staff College of India.

I.N.T.A.C.H., 1987. *The Tehri Dam : A Prescription for Disaster.* Delhi

Iyer, R.R., 1989. "Large Dams : The Right Perspective", *EPW,* Vol. XXIV, No. 39, pp. A-107-16.

Jaine, Roberts, 1978. *From Massacre to Mining : The Colonisation of Aboriginal Australia.* London : CIMRA.

Jansen, Robert B., 1980. *Dams and Public Safety*. Washington, D.C. : US Deptt. of Interior.

Joshi, Vidyut, 1983. *Rehabilitation of Sub-merging Villages (General Report on Sardar Sarovar-Narmada Project)*. Surat : Centre for Social Studies.

Kannan, K.P., 1979. "Ecological and Socio-economic Consequences of Water-Control Projects in Kuttanad Region of Kerala", *Proc. Ind. Ac. Sc.*, Vol. C 2, Part 4, pp. 417-33.

Karia, H.J. and P.P. Oza, 1982. "Catastrophe of Dam-burst at Morvi (Gujarat) and Restoration of Water Supply System", *Jnl. of the I.W.W.A.*, Vol. XIV, No. 2, pp. 135-38.

Karve, I. and Jai Nimbkar, 1969. *A Survey of the People Displaced through the Koyna Dam*. Poona : Deccan College.

Lok Sabha Debate, 1955. *Calling Attention to Matter of Urgent Public Importance : Floods in Orissa*, 13 Sept.

Mahalanobis, P.C., 1932. *Rainstorms and River Floods in Orissa*. Revised Edn. 1941.

Mahapatra, L.K., 1990, "Rehabilitation of Tribals Affected by Major Dams and other Projects in Orissa." in A.P. Fernandez (ed), *A Report on the Workshop on Rehabilitation of Person Displaced by Development Projects*. Bangalore : Institute for Social and Economic Change and Myrada.

Mahapatra, L.K., 1991. "Development for Whom? Depriving the Dispossessed Tribals". *Social Action*, Vol. 41, No. 3, pp. 271-87.

Mankodi, Kashyap and T. Gangopadhyay, 1983. *Rehabilitation : The Economic and Ecological Costs*. Surat : Centre for Social Studies.

Mankodi, Kashyap, 1986. "Appraisal of Resettlement and Rehabilitation", *Training Workshop on Technical Analysis of Dams*, Udaipur.

Mark, R.K. and D.E, Stuart, 1997. "Disasters as a Necessary Part of Benefit-Cost Analysis", *Science*, Vol. 197, pp. 160-62.

Misra, B., 1947. "Land Tenure in the District of Sambalpur", *Indian Journal of Agricultural Economics*, Vol. 27, Part-II.

Mitra, Ashok K., 1989. "Mounting Antagonism towards Big Dams", *EPW*, Vol. XXIV, No. 31, p. 1791.

Mohan, Dinesh, 1989. "Promotion of Modern Technology : A New Tool for Neo-Colonialism", *EPW*, Vol. XXIV, pp. 1815-18.

Mohanty, Kamdeb. 1981. "The Impact of Indravati Dam Project on the Life of the Citizens of the Area", paper presented at the Special Seminar on *Upper Indravati Project : Development and Human Problems*. Bhubaneshwar. Utkal University, Deptt. of Anthropology (unpublished).

Mohapatra, Chittaranjan. 1981. "Foreseeable Problems of Displacement : Indravati Dam Project as a Factor", paper presented at the Special Seminar on *Upper Indravati Project : Development and Human Problems*. Bhubaneshwar. Utkal University, Deptt. of Anthropology (unpublished).

Nanda, S. and P.K. Tripathy, 1987. 'The Hirakud Rehabilitation and the Displaced People', *Seminar on Development and Displacement*, Centre for Study of Culture and Society, Burla, 20-21 Dec.

N.C.H.S.E., 1986. *Documentation on Rehabilitation of Displaced Persons due to Construction of Major Dams*. Delhi.

Pant, C. and S. Dharmadhikary, 1989. "Mounting Antagonism towards Big Dams", *EPW*, Vol. XXIV, Nos. 35&36, pp. 2035-36.

Paranjpye, Vijay, 1980. *Pawana Dam and Bedki Hydel Project in Karnataka*. Delhi : Gandhi Peace Foundation Centre.

Paranjpye, Vijay, 1988. *Evaluating the Tehri Dam : An Extended Cost-Benefit Appraisal*, N. Delhi: INTACH.

Patnaik, S.C., 1968. "Irrigation Rates in Orissa : How Commercial should they be?" *EPW*, Vol. III, No. 22, pp. 839-42.

Patnaik, S.K., B. Das and A. Mishra, 1987. "Hirakud Dam Project : Expectation and Reality," Paper presented at a *Workshop on People and Dams*. New Delhi : Society for Participatory Research in Asia", Sept. 14-18.

Punalekar, S.P., 1984. "Voluntary Action and Rehabilitation : A Case of Narmada Dam Oustees in Gujarat State", *Indian Journal of Social Work*, Vol. XLV, No. 2.

Ramachandran, K. K., 1985. *Longterm Environmental and Ecological Impacts of Multi-purpose River valley Projects* (mimeo). Trivandrum : Centre for Earth Science Studies.

Rao, M.K., 1985. "Cracks in Hirakud Dam not repaired", *Free Press Journal*, Bombay, Feb. 13.

Ray, K.B., 1955. "Flood Damages of 1955", *Economic Weekly*, Vol. 11, No. 41, pp. 1197-99.

Redclift, Michael, 1984. *Development and the Environmental Crisis : Red or Green Alternatives*. London and New York : Methuen.

Reddy, U.B., 1988. "Impact of Large irrigation projects on the tribals", *Social change*, Vol. 18, No. 1.

Rodrigues, Denis, 1989. "Rallying against Planned Disaster", *EPW*, Vol. XXIV, p. 2183.

Samuel, Ike, 1989. "Alarming rate of mortality", *Indian Express*, New Delhi, Feb. 24, p. 10.

Sarangi, S. and R. Billorey, 1988. "The Nightmare Begins": Oustees of Indira Sagar Project", *EPW*, 23 Apr, pp. 829-30 .

Sarin, Akash, 1983. "Rajasthan : A Disastrous Scheme", *Probe India*, June, pp. 46-49.

Satrughna, M., 1981. "Unrehabilitated poor of the Srisailam Project", *EPW*, Dec.26, pp. 2123-26.

Sawant, P.R., 1985. *River Dam Construction and Resettlement of Affected Villages : A Case Study of Two villages in the Upper Krishna Valley : Vyakali and Chandavadi (Distt. Satara)*. Delhi : Inter-India.

Scudder, Thayer, 1985. "A Sociological Framework for the Analysis of New Land Settlements", In M.M. Cernea (ed), *Putting People First : Sociological Variables in Rural Development*. New York : OUP.

SEAI, 1987. *Irrigation Projects in Social and Economic Atlas of India*. Delhi : Oxford University Press.

Sen, Badal, 1981. "Economics of Dams", *Frontier*, Nov. 7, pp. 11-13.

Sengupta Nirmal, 1985. *Irrigation : Traditional Vs. Modern*. Madras : Madras Institute of Development Studies.

Sethi, Sunil, 1983. "Vishnu Prayag Project : Blue Print for Disaster", *India Today*, Nov.30, pp. 142-143.

Sharma, L.T. and Ravi Sharma (eds), 1981. *Major Dams : A Second Look : Development without Destruction*. Delhi; Gandhi Peace Foundation.

Sharma, Sudhirender, 1985. "The Case against Big Dams", *Indian Express*, Feb. 17.

Sikka, D.R., 1987. "Guidelines for Resettlement and Rehabilitation of Uprooted Agricultural Population in River Valley Projects", *Pong Dam Oustees (Documents)*. Delhi : MARG.

Simpson, D.W., 1976. "Seismicity Change Associated with Reservoir Loading", *Engineering Geology*, Vol. 10, No. 2, pp. 123-50.

Singh, Satyajit K., 1990. "Evaluating Large Dams in India", *EPW*, Vol. XXV, No. 11, pp. 561-7.

Sinha, B.N., 1971. *Geography of Orissa*. Delhi : National Book Trust.

Skaria, Ajay, 1985. "The Narmada Project : Valley of the Dammed", *Indian Express*. Feb. 17.

Smith, Norman, 1971. *A History of Dams*. London : Peter Davies.

Sovani, N.V. and N. Rath, 1960. *Economics of a Multiple-purpose River Dam : Report of an inquiry into the Economic benefits of the Hirakud Dam*. Pune : G.I.P.E.

Staff Correspondent, 1957. "Hirakud Dam Supplement", *The Times of India*, 13 Jan. pp. 13-17.

Staff Correspondent, 1981. "Srisailam Project : A Forced Exodus", *India Today*, July 16-31, pp. 52-55.

Staff Correspondent, 1982. "Karnataka : Natural Calamity That was Not," *Link*, Jan 31, pp 22-23.

Staff Correspondent, 1987. "Hirakud Dam defects pointed out", *Indian Express*, 20 July.

Staff Correspondent, 1987. "Hirakud Dam fast silting up", *Indian Express*, 25 Aug.

Staff Correspondent, 1987. "Pollutants damage Hirakud Dam", *Indian Express*, 8 Jun.

Staff Correspondent, 1988. "Hirakud dam — Orissa's curse", *The Hindustan Times*, Nov. 29, p.3.

Staff Correspondent, 1989. "High death rate of Narmada Oustees", *The Times of India*, N. Delhi, March 9, p.8.

Staff Correspondent, 1989. "A People's dam in Sangli", *The Times of India*, New Delhi, Mar. 29, p.1.

Staff Correspondent, 1989. "Next WB loan to Narmada after review", *The Times of India*, New Delhi, Apr. 28, p.7.

Staff Correspondent, 1989. "Bungling in Narmada Works", *Indian Express*, New Delhi, Mar 27, p.10.

Staff Correspondent, 1989. "Discharges from dams led to floods", *The Statesman*, New Delhi, Aug. 7, p.7.

Supakar, Shraddhakar, 1988. *Itihasara Parihasa* (Oriya). Sambalpur : Trimurti.

Survival International, 1985(a). "India : The Narmada Dam Project (Communication with the World Bank)", May, pp. 1-8.

Survival International, 1985(b). "India : World Bank Violates International Law", Oct.

Temple, Richard, 1864. *Report on the Mahanuddy and its Tributaries*. Calcutta : John G. Hirons.

The Economic Times (Mid-Week Review), 1989. "Sardar Sarovar, Narmada", Sept. 28.

Tucker, Richard, 1984. "High Dams and Forests : Building Environmental Alliances in India", *Sierra Magazine*, March-April pp. 1-13.

Viegas, Philip, 1991. "The Hirakud Dam Oustees : Thirty Years After", in *Rivers of Joy, Rivers of Change*, Delhi : Multiple Action Research Group.

Vohra, B.B., 1987. "Managing India's Water Resources : Land Management holds the key", Key Note Address, *National Seminar of National Association of Water Development Agencies.* Hyderabad, 12 August.

INDEX